# TRAPPED

T0043446

# TRAPPED

## A True Story

*A MOTHERS'S SEARCH FOR THE TRUTH
IN THE WAKE OF UNSPEAKABLE TRAGEDY*

By Dana Danuta Banat

**TATE PUBLISHING**
AND ENTERPRISES, LLC

Published by Tate Publishing & Enterprises, LLC
127 E. Trade Center Terrace | Mustang, Oklahoma 73064 USA
1.888.361.9473 | www.tatepublishing.com

Tate Publishing is committed to excellence in the publishing industry. The company reflects the philosophy established by the founders, based on Psalm 68:11,
*"The Lord gave the word and great was the company of those who published it."*

Book design copyright © 2015 by Tate Publishing, LLC. All rights reserved.
*Cover design by Junriel Boquecosa*
*Interior design by Jomel Pepito*

Published in the United States of America

ISBN: 978-1-68028-800-1
1. Family & Relationships / Death, Grief, Bereavement
2. Religion / Christian Life / Death, Grief, Bereavement
15.03.09

# Contents

In honor of God's glory
and in memory of my beloved daughter Lisa.
Genesis 1-1, "In the beginning God
created the heavens and earth."


Most of the people's names and some places
mentioned in this book were changed.

# AKNOWLEDGMENTS

## THANK YOU TO MY HUSBAND, BERNARD...

I can think of no better person on Earth, my love—you are my supporter for better or worse. When I wrote the song "springtime," I was thinking of our love, which is still strong in my heart. You inspired me to write this song:

*You are always, for me, the one*
*Love takes more and never is done*
*And God's promise is our guide,*
*Still it is right, still it is right.*
*How many years we've faced different trials?*
*Together, together, we walk through the fire.*

I thank God for you, day and night, and you are always in my prayers. I trust God with our future now and forever.

## THANK YOU TO MY SON, PETER...
You have gone with us through the most difficult journey in our lives. I am thankful to God for you. Watching your faith in God grow makes me very happy for you. You and Lisa are the most beautiful gifts and the greatest blessings given to us by God. You are so special, and the best son I could ever dream of. You have a wonderful heart, full of love, faithfulness and responsibility. You and your future family are always in my prayers, and I know that you are in God's hands and he will guide you and protect you, now and forever.

## THANK YOU TO MY SISTER, JOLA...

You showed me love and courage in the most tragic
moment of my life. You were patient, gentle and
kind, and you were always ready to support me
in pursuing whatever ideas I came up with.
You have a heart like a mountain! I am
very blessed to have a sister like you.
We are more than sisters; we are the best friends ever.
I thank God for you and have you always in my prayers.

## THANK YOU TO THE EASTON BAPTIST CHURCH...

Thank you so much for supporting me in my time
of grief. I am especially thankful to my "sunshine"
sisters. Thank you for your wonderful help; I know
that I can count on you. You are wonderful friends
with courage and kindness. I am blessed to be a part
of this church family. I thank God and pray for you.

## THANK YOU TO MY NEW YOUNG FRIEND, LAUREN...

For your compassion and understanding, and for
always being ready to help me anytime I need it, even
when you are busy with your own life. You were my
first, wonderful editor for this book, but you were also
my neighbor who knew my daughter Lisa, and this
connection was special for us when we worked on
this  book together. Your lovely personality and very
positive, enthusiastic energy was good for me at this
hard time of my life.  I thank God and pray for you.

THANK YOU TO MY DAUGHTER LISA'S CLOSE FRIENDS: AMANDA, NIELLE, CAROL, JONI, and ASHLEY... for your wonderful stories and encouragement in my time of grief, and for still remembering me. A special thanks to Amanda who grew up with Lisa and had a close relationship with her—it was as if you two were sisters. Amanda grieves with me deeply, and does the best she can to remember her. I thank God and pray for you all.

THANK YOU TO ALL OUR FRIENDS AND NEIGHBORS... who during my family's tragedy came to our house with compassion and food. Thank you also for all the support from Lisa's teachers, friends from Mansfield High School, and all who sent us cards and flowers. I thank God and pray for you.

THANK YOU TO GOD FOR MY BELOVED DAUGHTER LISA...
It was the best time of my life to care for her and for my family. She was a special blessing to our family, who brought us so much laughter and happiness. She always had a beautiful, open heart that loved and cherished others, and genuinely cared. She was always hopeful and taught us how to appreciate and be joyful, even from the little tiny things.

# The News

## In Search of Freedom

July 15, 2012, was the day that changed everything.

I had a strange dream that night: I was someplace dark, like a cemetery perhaps, with my mother who had passed away twenty years before. She wanted to show me something. She told some man to dig out her grave and open it, but when I looked down into it, the grave was empty. She then pointed to a fresh grave nearby and ordered him to dig there too. It was also empty.

I was confused. I asked her, "Whose grave is this?" But she did not answer me.

"They are empty," she said. "We are not here. Don't look for us in these places."

When I woke up at six o'clock, I was surprised to see the time. I had been in the habit of waking up at four for many years. It was unusual for me to wake up so much later than normal, and I felt uneasy. The dream had been dreadful, and I couldn't stop thinking about it.

*What does it mean?* I wondered. Many years before, I had dreamed about my mother being in heaven. It was a glorious vision, and after it, I stopped dreaming about her altogether... until that night. It stayed on my mind as I made my bed and started my day.

As I walked to the bathroom to take a shower, I heard the front doorbell ring. *Who would come so early?* I thought *maybe my daughter Lisa forgot her key,* so I rushed downstairs to open the door.

*What are the police doing here?* I wondered. *And why are there so many of them? Did something happen?* I looked at them, waiting for someone to speak, not understanding why they had come. I noticed the chaplain was with them when he suddenly turned from his back to the front, and he looked as if he was acting. For a while, he looked into my eyes, not saying anything and waiting. I started crying, and one of the state police troopers began to explain what had happened.

*Communism has collapsed!* For years we had lived in fear, with the government controlling every aspect of our lives. Our mail was opened and reviewed. Our calls were monitored. We had to be careful about what we said on the phone, or our calls could be forcibly disconnected. We were watched at school, at work, in any public place. Officials could stop us any time to ask where we were going and why. We had to get permission and have an explanation when we wanted to visit our family in neighboring countries. There was no privacy and no freedom. The communist regime sought to control everything, from our beliefs to how much we could own. People did not trust each other because everyone lived in fear. Corruption was everywhere. We felt hopelessly trapped in this controlling and humiliating system.

And then God answered our prayers and saved Poland from another horrible war. Because of our trust in God, we lived to see the end of communism in 1989. What we had once thought impossible had happened; the snare had been broken, and we were free. We could finally make our own choices.

In 1980, through a wave of strikes, ("Solidarity" anticommunist trade union and social movement) Poland's communist government allowed some people who did not agree with them to emigrate. About this time, in 1987, we were in Germany with thousands of other Polish people. We were waiting to immigrate to a foreign country with greater opportunities for us. We wanted to start a new life. The process of waiting was humiliating. We had to move from one refugee camp to another and from one city to another, every time being aggressively interviewed about our status. Going through this process was very difficult for my husband and me and for our five-year-old son, Peter. We worried constantly about our uncertain future, but we held onto hope that it would be bright. At this time, we had the choice of whether to immigrate to Australia, Canada, or the United States. We wanted to go to the US. My younger brother, Mark, was already there with his wife, Sylvia, waiting for us.

In the past, we had visited them as tourists, and I fell in love with the freedom in the country. I could talk freely without being ashamed of my language, and the people seemed friendly; even strangers smiled at me. I was also impressed by how huge everything was: stores, homes, cars, factories, cities. Everything was overflowing with wealth like I'd never seen before. It was more beautiful, with cleaner air to breathe. Most importantly, there was an amazing feeling of safety and the promise of a better life and future. America was like a dream, a promised land. I thought *it was the best land in the word.*

To wait for the decision of whether or not we could immigrate there was very frustrating, like "To be or not to be." Our fortune, whether it was to be good or bad, was in their hands. We had nothing. We risked everything, but we believed it was worth it. We were still young and had hopes, dreams, and plans for our future. From time to time, we got calls from one of the immigration offices or an embassy to set us up with a medical examination or interview. After each one of those meetings, our spirits were lifted, but as more time passed, our stress increased and fear gripped us. How long would we have to wait to be free? Who would take us?

Two insecure years passed, and we learned that the US was not taking any more immigrants.

We still hoped that Australia or Canada would take us, and after another interview, we were accepted to Australia. I was so excited that I wanted to give away our warm winter jackets and all of our warm clothes. It would be hard to take them with us when most flights only allowed fifty pounds of luggage per person. Fifty pounds would be all we could carry from our old lives to our new country. But my husband didn't want me to get rid of the winter clothes yet.

"We are still not sure that we are 100 percent going to Australia," he said. And he was right. We had more waiting ahead of us, so we could not get rid of our coats. I wanted to believe that we were going to Australia and this nightmare would be over.

We were tired of waiting long and of being homeless foreigners in Germany, without a country or work; lack of security was very burdensome. We worried about the future, about money, about our son who struggled to learn

German in school. Thank God we were healthy and could care for each other. Love and hope kept us strong.

At this time, I observed that my husband's faith was increasing tremendously. He was looking for God, and he often took us to church, where he prayed earnestly.

Another few months passed by without any more word on Australia. Our son had just finished first grade at the elementary school in Germany when we got good news. Canada called us for a new interview, and it seemed likely we'd be able to move there. Right around the same time, more good news came. We found out that America was still considering our application.

One day, when we were at the small chapel we often went to, my husband, Ben, pulled Peter and I aside.

"Listen to me," he said. "Do you agree with me? We will trust God. Whichever one of these countries will take us first is where we will go, even if we hear from America right in the same day. We will trust God, okay? We will go to wherever comes first."

Peter and I agreed, and Ben said a prayer for our family. He prayed to God to give us the strength to trust Him with His choice for us, wherever it would be, and he asked God to give him work so that he would be able to provide for us. We left it up to God and trusted Him with our future. Though I promised my husband that I would trust God with the decision, I really hoped that America would come through first.

I admired Ben's foundation of faith because it never seemed to weaken. My husband was brought up in a good Catholic family. They had a nice home with a cozy garden. His father was a farmer, and his family was busy working hard. His mother was an especially strong believer. I, on the other hand, was raised mostly in an orphanage. My father was in prison for seven years, and then later, he remarried. This happened when I was three years old, my sister was two, and my brother was newborn baby. My mother was left alone with three small kids at age eighteen. She was as vulnerable as teenagers could be. During World War II, she was born to a family with seven children. She was the youngest, and by a very early age, she had to learn to take care of herself. She started working before she was sixteen, lying that she was eighteen. One time working the second shift, she went home from work alone late at night; she was raped, became pregnant, and then she miscarried. After that, she met my father, who was in the military and was much older than my mom. They married and after a few years of living together, my father was arrested, then sent to prison. When my mother was left alone, she had nobody to help her. I believe that she was bitter and angry. Our teen mom was not responsible enough to take care of us and of herself. We often were abused, hungry, and cold. Later, when I became a mother, my mom and I became very good friends. I learned from my stepfather that she'd died suddenly at the age fifty five; she was reading the Bible and was meeting Jehovah's witnesses. I thank God with all my heart for that, and I knew she was saved. Before I became a Christian, my faith wavered, and I found it hard to steadily trust in God.

In the orphanage, under the communist system, we were forbidden to go to church or talk about God, so I trusted my husband because of his strong faith.

Those days waiting to emigrate from Germany were dull, dragging one after another. Waiting was stressful and exhausting, and we had chosen to leave a lot behind when we left Poland. Early in our marriage, my husband spent a few years working in Patagonia, Argentina. We were forced to spend two of those years apart from each other because the government would not allow us both to leave Poland. At that time, many people were escaping to foreign countries to escape from the harsh communist system. To keep us from fleeing the country, my husband's salary was held in Poland, and we were told that it would be paid upon our return. We only got enough money for our food every week. We lived in a work camp, so we didn't have to pay for an apartment. By deciding not to return to Poland, we knew we would lose everything. The urge to start again in a completely new land, where we could make our own choices, was naturally stronger in us than the desire for just repayment of our hard-earned money.

Finally, it happened. We got the news! We were going to Canada. Wow, was I glad to have kept our warm jackets and clothes. We would need them!

We got a call from the American embassy too. They told us to be patient, and I was tempted to wait.

But Ben said, "We've prayed, and we will trust God! We are going to Canada!"

At this time of my life, I did not know the Bible. Now I would sing Psalm 125:1 (NLT), "Those who trust in the Lord are as secure as Mount Zion; they will not be defeated but will endure forever."

## America: The Promise Land

I command you—be strong and courageous! Do not
be afraid or discouraged.
For the Lord your God is with you
wherever you go.

—Joshua 1:9 (NLT)

Embarking on a new beginning was exciting and scary.

Ben learned English by himself and only took a few English lessons. He always learned new languages fast. He already fluently spoke Spanish, French, and German. Our son, Peter, also learned quickly, but I found English to be very difficult. I knew I would have trouble with it.

I think that growing up mostly in an orphanage caused me to develop very low self-esteem, which doesn't help anyone who is trying to learn anything. Much later, when I became a Christian, it took God a long time to fix me.

Our arrival in Canada was a miraculously smooth transition. Before we came to Canada, my lovely sister-in-law, Sylvia, called a priest in Canada to help us. One of the nuns from Sylvia's church in America recommended Father Jim as a sponsor for us. He was old and did not hear well.

Sylvia told me that there was a bad phone connection when she spoke with Father Jim. It turns out he misunderstood her when she used the word *sister*. He thought that my sister-in-law was a nun because nuns are also called sister, and Father Jim's priority was to sponsor and help clergies' families first.

We did not know anybody in Canada, so we were thankful to God that He worked through my sister-in-law to help us start our new lives. We had no money for a hotel but some for food.

It was a wonderful blessing that Father Jim came to pick us up from the airport on that cold, rainy day when we arrived. It was a miracle that he rented an apartment for us and paid up front for our first three months of rent. It was small but nice and furnished, and it was a miracle that food was in the refrigerator when we moved in.

Despite all these incredible blessings, beginning to live in Canada was not easy. We did not have a car, Ben spoke poor English, and we were not ready for the severe winter.

But we had our permanent resident cards, and after three years, we could become citizens. We had hoped that things would only improve for us. We loved each other, and the hardship only made our relationship stronger.

At first, we struggled to find jobs, enroll Peter in school, and learn English. My husband's faith and his trust in God changed those hardships into blessings, and I learned from him to see them as such. If we had not immigrated to Canada, he would not have had the opportunity to work for International Nickel Company in Sudbury, which was one of the first in the world to computerize their technology on such a large scale. It wasn't an accident that they needed Ben to quickly get his license through Professional Engineers Ontario (PEO). He gained tremendous engineering experience as a result.

After two years of living in Canada, we rented a nice, comfortable two-bedroom apartment. We bought an old but nice car, and Ben had a respectable job. Life became more stable, and we started to enjoy it. We took advantage of the winters by skiing, skating, and playing in the snow. We made plans for our future there, counting down the months until we would become citizens. We embraced our freedom in Canada. We did not feel any pressure of the rules we had lived with under communism. We could make our own choices about how and where to live. We could say and believe what we wanted to believe—if we were followers of Christ, we weren't discriminated against. But it wasn't all easy. With this freedom came new financial responsibility: medical care, insurance, saving for retirement and for putting our children through college, and making smart investments. The custom from our old communist country—that whether I work or I don't, I get the reward—did not exist here. We had to plan carefully for our future, and even thoughts of becoming sick and not being able to work were horrifying. We were free as birds let out of a cage. Now we just had to watch out for hunters.

Winter in Sudbury was severe and long. We missed our family in America. I miss my younger brother Mark and his wife Sylvia. We always had fun with them. The times we spent together were full of jokes and laughter, and we hadn't seen them for quite some time.

When spring came and we only had three months left to become citizens of Canada, we were shocked to find a permit in the mail from the American embassy, giving us permission to immigrate to the US. We were baffled as to how they could have found us in Canada and why they had bothered. On top of that, the permit only gave us three months to move from Canada. We asked ourselves, "Is this a coincidence?" We hesitated; in America, we'd need to wait five years to be eligible for citizenship. Plus, Ben had just started his successful career, and everything was going so well in Canada. We had a difficult decision to make. We prayed and waited for some sign from God. We were not sure if we should move.

Spring and autumn are my favorite seasons because life changes seem to happen the most at this time.

By the start of May, we only had one month left to make a choice. Our family from America was encouraging us to come, and I started to remind myself how much I loved their freedom and the easy American lifestyle. Everything seemed possible in this admirable big country. There was room for even bigger dreams and opportunities. But most importantly, I liked the idea of being closer to my family. We missed them very much.

Anxiety continued to grow as we neared our decision deadline, until my husband's birthday at the end of May. We had planned to go out to a restaurant to celebrate, but that day, there was a beautiful snowstorm, and we had to stay home.

Bright blue sky and sunlight were showing through gray cloud that poured large snowflakes down upon us. Thunder was shaking the earth, and the wind was spirited, howling continuously.

Peter and I were amazed. We watched the spectacular show from the window. Ben was watching TV in silence. Occasionally, he would look over at us when the thunder growled and caused us to squeak with excitement.

Peter and I kept shouting, "Wow!" as each flash of powerful lightning stroked the sky. But Ben wasn't interested in watching the storm with us. He wasn't content to have to celebrate his birthday at home watching TV instead of going to the restaurant. The storm lasted about an hour, and when it stopped, everything was covered with white snow glistening in the sun. A rainbow appeared in the sky, which was now perfectly blue.

I will never forget this birthday.

"That's it!" Ben said when the storm was finished. "It is my birthday. There should not be snow on my birthday. It's the end of May." Then we moved to America.

The beginning in America wasn't easy, but we were better prepared after our experience in Canada.

Despite how hard relocating always was for us, Peter adapted easily everywhere we went. He never complained and quickly learned many new things, such as skiing, swimming, and skating, on his own. He liked individual sports like karate, and we were always sure that he could belong to a good karate club. At school, he was a good student, very disciplined and very mature for his age.

Though Ben got a good job, we were constantly wrestling with money and were forced to follow it. First, my husband's company moved us to Houston, Texas, then to Gaithersburg, Maryland, which I liked a lot. We always thanked God for His care, His protection, and the blessings He gave us during these tough times. Ben took us to church every Sunday, but we only prayed in church or when we felt we needed it. I did not understand many of the religious traditions that Ben was practicing. Confession, rosary beads, praying to the saints, and other religion custom. All of these things were foreign to me, but I never asked about them. I was ashamed and embarrassed by my lack of knowledge.

I did believe in God, but I did not have any relationship with Him, at least I didn't think I did. Sometimes, I felt that I had a connection with God, but I wasn't sure how that could be.

While in Maryland twelve years after my first child, Peter, was born, I got pregnant for the second time. We planned this child. It had never been the right time before to have more children, but now, it felt like a dream come true. In Poland, the prevalent belief is that women should not get pregnant after age thirty-five. I was thirty-four, so I figured this would probably be the last chance for me. I knew that this baby would be healthy and special. I prayed to have a girl, and my gut told me that a girl was what I was having. I dreamed and prayed about what she would be like—healthy, smart, pretty, tall, blond, and sweet. I was overjoyed. When I was pregnant, we moved again; this time to Boston, Massachusetts. I wanted to stay in Maryland, but I was also looking forward to being so close to Mark and Sylvia, who also lived in Boston. Ben promised that the project would only last for a few years and said that then, more than ever, we needed to be close with our family because we were expecting our second child. Ben got a job working on the Big Dig in Boston, and we rented a nice two-bedroom apartment on the eighth floor of a complex in the center of Quincy, just opposite from Peter's middle school. It was convenient for Ben too. He only had a short walk to the T, which took him right to work in ten minutes. Life became organized and promising.

## The Vision: Jesus's Face

The Lord says, "I will guide you along the best pathway for your life. I will advise you and watch over you."

—Psalm 32:8 (NLT)

I knew the baby would be big. My belly was huge, but I was feeling good and happy. Ben, however, seemed depressed.

I assumed that he was having a hard time at work. At the time, I did not know what he was going through, and we weren't communicating as well as usual. It seemed as if he had no time for me anymore. He often had to work on weekends, and he came home very late from his job. I know now that communication between us was tough because he faced massive stress at work, but because I was pregnant, he didn't want to upset me by talking about it. He explained to me later how hard it was. At the time, we only had a green card, and we had to wait for five years for our citizenship. He felt pressured to work much harder and stay longer at work than others to gain trust and respect for his work ethic, so that is what he did. At the time, though, not knowing exactly what was going on caused me to become depressed. I loved him, and the lack of any sign of love from him was killing me. I felt hopeless and alone and disappointed. We were free from the pressure of communism, and this should bring more happiness into our life. We were in a foreign country struggling to live in a completely new culture. This brought a new set of challenges and issues to deal with. I needed God more than ever.

As a child, I grew up in an orphanage located in a nice old mansion. When I was about seven years old, every Sunday, I would wait for my mom to come and visit me. All day, I would sit on the staircase in front of the main entrance, sometimes without any break for eating or using the bathroom, to be sure I would not miss her. But she never visited me. I made a vow that I would never do to my own children what she had done; I would never drink alcohol or get a divorce. I would love my family and be there for my children. I would love them no matter what I had to go through. I would love them.

When I made that vow from the deepest desire of my heart, I realized what I was waiting for all those Sundays— it was love.

I never forgot my childhood vow. It was as if I had put a seal on my heart. It is always there. But now I felt disillusioned and even sorry that I had made this vow. I wondered what was wrong with me. I loved my family. I loved my husband, son, and this new baby in me for which I had waited twelve years. I loved them more than anything in this world, but I still felt this insatiable hunger for love. I didn't understand how this could be. Didn't I have a son and husband? Wasn't I pregnant? Isn't that enough?

But my depression grew the busier Ben became. It was another long lonely evening at home, and I looked through the window often, hoping to see Ben marching home. It was almost dark. I was so disappointed that I hid my face in the curtain and cried, praying to God with all my heart, *Please, help me to be sure that you really exist, that you really love me, that I can love you too.*

*Please, God, I want to know. I want to be sure that you are real.*

Still crying at the window, I heard a voice in my head ask, *Do you really want this?* It was not my own inner voice but something else entirely. At this moment, I had a strong feeling that a lot would change depending on my answer and it would not be easy, but I thought, *What do I have to lose?*

*Yes, I want this*, I responded.

The voice returned. *Wait. Something will happen*, it said.

After that, I felt peaceful. I wondered what would happen. I was excited and curious. What? Where? When? How long would I have to wait? The feeling of peace did not leave me, and I realized then how little I knew about

God. I wanted to know everything I could. I wanted to read the Bible and know God. As fast as I could, I ordered two Bibles—one in English and one in Polish—and then I waited for my sign. All my worries faded to nothing when I heard that voice so full of reassurance. I felt secure that God is in control.

Later, during another one of those lonely evenings, the baby suddenly stopped moving. Usually, she stirred in my belly all the time and kept me awake at night. I thought, *Finally, I can go to bed early and get a good night's rest.* Moments after lying down, I closed my eyes and slowly drifted away. Not long after I had fallen asleep, a light woke me. I was too tired to open my eyes right away and also a little annoyed that I was disturbed from my sleep so soon. I wondered who had turned the light on in my room. I felt as if somebody was looking at me.

With my eyes still closed, I began thinking, *Maybe Ben has come home and is checking on me.* But it was too quiet, and I didn't feel the presence of any person or any sound of breathing or movement. After waiting in vain for the light to be turned off, I finally opened my eyes to investigate.

I froze immediately. What I saw was beyond my comprehension. On the same curtain where I had cried to God in earnest and asked Him for a sign, I saw the face of Jesus Christ surrounded by soft white light. He was looking at me, slowly tilting His head from one side to another with such an expression of love in His face that it was overwhelming. The face was similar to the picture in church. I heard in my head over and over, *I love you. I love you. I love you.*

I felt guilty and embarrassed. I knew that what I felt was a pure kind of love, which I had never known or experienced before.

While my tension grew, I simultaneously felt a calm reassurance to not be afraid.

This love was too much for me to uphold. It was overpowering my emotions and challenging my understanding. Somehow, I knew that he would stay for as long as I needed, but I felt overwhelmingly that I couldn't bear this love any longer and it had to leave. The vision slowly faded like ripples on water, and it was dark once more. I was so exhilarated and awake that I wondered how I was supposed to fall asleep after that. But somehow, I did, and this was the last thought that I remembered. When I woke up late the next morning, I was surprised. It felt as if I had just closed my eyes and soon opened them. I felt extremely well rested—more, I thought, *than I ever had,* as if I had just awoken from being unconscious or from being under anesthesia. Completely revived, I sat on my bed thinking about what had happened. It was Saturday, my new beginning.

I did not believe in visions before this. I had always been a skeptic. Now that I had experienced one for myself, I had to accept what I had seen. I knew it would be difficult to keep a secret, but I doubted if anyone, even Ben, would believe me. Ben noticed a change in me and was curious as to what had caused it. I did not care anymore how late he came home from work. I was always content, joyful, and peaceful, and I was reading the Bible with passionate enthusiasm.

After a month of this, Ben finally asked, "Why are you reading a Bible? Do you want to be a nun?"

I laughed. "No, I want to know God." Then despite my fear that he wouldn't believe me, I told him what had happened.

"I believe you," he said.

"I am the way and the truth and the life. No one comes to the Father except through me…Anyone who has seen me has seen the Father."

—John 14:6, 9 (NLT)

Shortly after that, on a sunny and warm spring day, our daughter, Lisa, was born. She was delivered naturally—a perfectly healthy, beautiful baby girl. She was big, full of energy, and exceptionally easy. I did not have any sleepless nights with her. She was always smiling, never fussy with food, and she never gave me any trouble with her health. I loved and adored my beautiful happy Lisa. She was born on May 13, 1993. Most people think thirteen is an unlucky number, but I believe it is the number of love. In the Bible, 1 Corinthians 13, "Love is the Greatest," is the most beautiful love poem I know. Later, it became Lisa's favorite too.

During our second year in America, when Lisa was still an infant, we moved into our first home. It was June of 1994, and the economy was good. It was the best time to take on a mortgage, so we did. Our development was new, just basic homes without additions or garages. Adjusting to life was not easy for us. It seemed to us that everything in America revolved around money and that people worked so hard so that they could have a lot of it. We noticed how our new neighbors competed with one another. When Ben spoke with them, he often mentioned building a new addition with a garage onto our home. We ended up changing our minds, but most of our neighbors added garages to their homes. Then they would ask Ben, "Where is your garage?"

At the time, Ben was working long hours, and I was raising our children, driving them to different activities, cooking, cleaning the house, doing the laundry, grocery shopping. I enjoyed being a mom and a caretaker. The Big Dig that Ben worked at in Boston became a long project, and we were happy to be able to raise our children in one place with peace.

After my vision, I had an inner need to stay connected with God. Through faith, I was learning to make the right choices in my life. Reading the Bible helped me to know God better. Many things had to be changed; however, God was patient with me.

After a while, I switched from a Catholic church to a Baptist one. Ben did not understand.

"Why do you want to change religions?" he asked.

"I'm not changing my religion," I replied. "Just the 'style.' Because the US is a free country. Everybody has a style!" There was a huge variety of churches available here, even strange ones like Scientology or Satanism; some of them I couldn't even understand, but people were free to choose. At the time when I lived in Poland, I think that over 90 percent were Catholic churches. It was tradition that every child be baptized; hence, I got baptized as well. I like my name. It was very popular in my country, and I got it because of the movie that was very famous at that time when my mom was pregnant with me. My name was so common that I had to have a different nickname. Officially, I would be called Danuta. For a small cute girl, it would be Danusia; if somebody did not like me, it would be Danka. The one that I like the most—because only close friends would call me this—was Dana; it was rare and special. When I came to the USA, my name Danuta was very unique, and I was proud of it, but I was surprised that Dana was ordinary here. So when I change from Catholic to Baptist Church, I was happy to find out that I could be baptized like Jesus was, and could choose a name. I struggled to decide which name I should pick. I like now my unique name—Danuta, and I recall how much I always wanted to be called Dana. It was amazing to me when early in the morning, the day of my and my daughter's baptism, I was awoken by a gentleman's voice. He called my name slowly, and I heard two times: *Dana…Dana.* Nobody was in my bedroom, and I knew it was God's voice. The name was chosen, and I felt ashamed. Then I realized that God loves me and He is my best friend.

My new Baptist church was a nice, normal, traditional church. The pastor there taught from passages of the Bible. It was in that church that my ten-year-old daughter Lisa and I acknowledged our salvation through Jesus Christ and were baptized on Easter of 2003. For the occasion, I had to choose a hymn for the ceremony; but at the time, I did not know many, so I decided to write one. I titled it "The Lord Is Alive" and set it to a simple march melody. It's become one of my favorite Easter hymns because the memory of the day was very special to me. To remember our baptism, Lisa and I designed two rings and had them made—gold for me and silver for her. On the top of each ring, we had "WWJD" engraved.

"The Lord Is Alive"

Dana Banat

The Lord is alive. All power is his.
Rejoice this Easter. Have guests and feast.
Rejoice! Give thanks! We're no longer slaves.
The power of love through Jesus has saved.

The Son of God, he showed the new way.
He rose from death. Alleluia, we pray.
He rose from death. Alleluia, we're saved!

We follow the Lord and learn his decrees.
With faith and hope, praise God with peace.
He chose and blessed us. We're no longer slaves.
The power of love through Jesus has saved.

The Son of God, he showed the new way.
He rose from death. Alleluia, we pray.
He rose from death. Alleluia, we're saved!

# The Storm

To follow you my God I fail and falter,
In every arise I see You brighter,
The hope in You is giving me strength,
My God, You know my very next step.

—D. B.

## Before the Storm

When we first arrived in the United States, I was amazed by how different everything was. Life seemed so smooth and easy. Most people were naturally at ease too. I noticed that food, however, was a top priority. Everyone was talking about it, and it seemed to be the main source of entertainment. At the beginning, it was quite an adjustment. Even at movie theaters, people were eating! In Europe at the time, eating at the cinema was absolutely forbidden. To do so would be considered incredibly rude, but here in the United States, everyone did it. It seemed that food was always on display no matter where I was. Many of the restaurants were different from anything I'd ever experienced. The restaurants with buffets were cheap, convenient, and fast, and the service there was only to clean up dirty dishes after the many meals you've eaten. I started enjoying this wonderful freedom. I began seeing the same names everywhere—McDonald's, Wendy's, Burger King, Dunkin' Donuts, Honeydew—and so many different pizza places almost on every corner. I was surprised to find that some of the "fast food" places even had big playgrounds for kids. When busy driving Peter and Lisa to their afterschool activities, the temptation to buy fast food was huge, especially because small toys always came with kid's meals. Sometimes, we would stop at one of these places to eat and play. It was hard to resist the amazing deals they would advertise—buy one burger get the second free—only in America! In Europe, food was much more expensive, and people usually preferred to feed their kids at home. "Take out" was making sandwiches at home to bring with you if there was no time to sit and eat. And people would only go to restaurants for special occasions. No one would ever dream of taking their leftovers because it wouldn't have been possible; food portions there were much smaller. And even if someone wanted to take food with them, they would probably be too embarrassed to ask because no place allowed it. Though there were some benefits to this, I now preferred the American attitude toward food. Here, I was given a choice. I could get bigger portions with the option to take home what I didn't finish, and I could have a break from cooking and enjoy more free time with my kids.

Shopping, I noticed, is also a huge source of entertainment. Nowhere in the world had I ever seen so many huge shopping malls; the ones here seemed enormous and bright like beautiful cathedrals.

Some of the stores play soothing music and smell like sweet perfume, and they tempt me, indulging my senses— "Come in."

So I do, only to look. But, wow, the big bright signs tell me everything is "ON SALE, TODAY ONLY," so I end up buying more than I need. Now I am late to get home. I am rushing with everything, upset that I spent too much money. I plan to return some of my purchases tomorrow—

half of it, I didn't even need—and now tomorrow, I will be tight on time too! This American lifestyle was very contagious, and I started to slowly adopt it.

Soon, I was unhappy to find that I'd gained weight even though I was very active in many sports. I didn't understand what I was doing wrong.

Just like seemingly everyone around me, I began talking about plans for dieting. I began to complain about the weather. "Isn't it too hot or too cold? Haven't we had enough rain already?" It was strange to notice myself developing different habits. In Poland, the weather was never something people spoke about other than when it was necessary. Our diets were never a topic of conversation either; we had enough food but never more than enough, so no one worried about becoming overweight. In some ways, these things were easier in Poland, but for me, America is a free country with a huge amount of opportunities and choices. Eventually, I learned that I didn't have to go with the flow. I could choose to live a healthy lifestyle even if unhealthy options were available. In America, like nowhere else, I believe it is possible with strength and faith to live a healthy and positive life.

As I slowly began to teach myself English, I started writing poems again. When I first started writing poems in preschool, I kept them hidden. I felt embarrassed by my inclination toward writing, so I kept it a secret. It was only after my vision of Jesus that I began to understand my style. God inspired my writing, and I had suspected when I was younger, that the poems I wrote sounded like song lyrics. I didn't believe that I would be good enough to learn to play some musical instrument.

When my daughter, Lisa, expressed an interest in learning how to play the piano, it was a pleasant surprise. She was eight years old, and it was right around the time I had begun to seriously write poetry again. I thought, *Maybe God has given her a gift.* We started going to a bigger church where they had much more music, and I felt it would be a perfect opportunity to share our talents.

I started writing songs, holiday hymns, and short performances based on the Bible, which Lisa played in church with others kids. She was my editor and helper. We always kept a small voice recorder with us because we never knew when an idea would come knocking.

One day when I was driving with her, she played the most beautiful song for me.

"Is it about me?" I asked her. "No, I feel this little light in me," she said, pointing to her chest. "It is about him."

I knew she was talking about Jesus. Lisa had shown me some poems and songs she had written, and they were very good. I knew she was blessed with a gift, and I encouraged her creativity. When she was teenager, though, some of our fellow church members discouraged her from continuing to sing or act. Every year, Lisa would go to a Christian camp with our church for a weekend; and one year, when she came back, she told me that she never wanted to go to youth group or to church anymore. I never found out the full story because she did not want to go into detail, but I knew she had been humiliated. The church leaders told her to sing something for fun, and later, they let everybody listen to it without her permission. Without her knowing, they had recorded her; and when they played it publicly, it sounded terrible, and everyone laughed at her. I tried my best to talk with her, but the damage was done, and she clearly needed time to heal. At around the same time, some of the church leaders wanted me to participate in an intensive Bible-study course. I was not able to commit to a year-long course at that time, so I was told I was no longer welcomed to perform in the church anymore. I was disappointed, but I understood that this kind of problem happened in many churches. In the New Testament especially, there are a lot of stories like that. Lisa and I talked to these church leaders and forgave them, but because of all these negative experiences, Lisa still tried to avoid church as much as possible. I eventually decided to return to the smaller church where Lisa and I had been baptized. Lisa still had faith and love for Jesus, and I knew she'd return in her own time. I tried to keep positive.

After my vision with Jesus's face, it was a surprise for me that it didn't matter what time I would go to sleep; every morning, I began waking up early, at around four o'clock, by myself. I spend these morning hours praying to God and reading the Bible. I love these peaceful moments of quiet meditation. They allow me to focus on having a positive outlook and prepare me to take a godly approach to any problems that come up during the day. It is not always easy and doesn't always work, but practice makes it a habit, and it gets easier. I still was trying to be active in church and do some plays and songs, but after Lisa became discouraged and did not want to do them with me, I lost my enthusiasm to glorify God. I decided to pray for her and just be patient and wait.

She was becoming a typical American teenager: working for money, hanging out with friends a lot, going to parties, and exercising at the gym. She did not have time to ride horses or play piano anymore even though she missed them very much. I understood she wanted to do the things that her friends were doing, but I also had faith she would return to church. I knew I just had to be patient. I had all of the comforts of an American life—the freedom to believe in what I wanted, eat as much as I wanted, dress how I wanted, and sleep in my cushy bed. *As long as that remained, I would be just fine.*

*Or so* I thought, until awakening day came.

## Accident, Crash, Trapped

> Jesus said: "My sheep recognized my voice; I know them, and they follow me. I give them eternal life, and they will never perish. No one will snatch them away from me, for my Father has given them to me, and he is more powerful than anyone else. So no one can take them from me. The Father and I are one."
>
> —John 10:27–30 (NLT)

Sunday morning, about six o'clock, July 15, 2012, I looked at the chaplain and started crying. *No, nothing happened. Calm down,* I was thinking.

I knew that everything the state trooper was saying was important, so I tried to be calm and listen.

"We think your daughter had an accident. Is she tall?" he asked.

"Yes," I heard myself answer.

"Does she have short hair?" he asked.

"Yes," I said again. I tried to avoid thinking negatively, and it was like I heard in my head, *It's important to be calm and listen.* "What happened?" I asked.

"Your daughter was killed by a driver going the wrong direction on Route 24 North. We don't know how he got there yet. Maybe he was speeding or driving the opposite direction on the highway. We suspect that he flipped over the Jersey barrier. We just don't know yet. It is still under investigation," he said. I was listening in disbelief to what he was talking about. "Your daughter is innocent. It isn't her fault," he assured me. I remember he repeated this a few times.

"It was a very weird car accident. A lot of cars were involved," he continued. "Including your daughter's car, four cars were crushed. Some ran away. Two were killed, but the other drivers are okay."

I remember staring at the officer's mouth; it was moving fast. I felt as if I were a student who hadn't been in school for a long time. I'd clearly missed some important lessons, and now that I needed to catch up, it was impossible to comprehend what was happening.

"What time did this happen?" I asked, surprised to hear my voice so calm.

"Before four o'clock. The night was completely dark. There were no known witnesses. No calls came in, and the other drivers had no idea what hit them. Everything happened so fast," he answered. "The man who killed your daughter died too. His pickup truck caught fire, and he was trapped inside, but the woman passenger who was with him survived, and she is okay."

"Who was this woman?" I asked, my voice shaking.

"We don't know," the state trooper replied.

"You don't *know*? You don't know who she is? Is she his wife?" I repeated with doubt.

The state trooper continued. "I don't know everything because I just came on my shift, but it's very weird. At that time, our officers had been chasing for a very long time a car all the way from Boston. We lost him in the Brockton area near Exit 18. We suspect that he ran away by driving the opposite direction on Route 24 north to Exit 15 toward Raynham. We suspect that he caused this accident."

"You were chasing a bad guy, and he killed my daughter?" I asked.

"No," he replied. "She was killed by the pickup truck who ended up driving the wrong way. There are a lot of things we still aren't sure about, like if she walked out of her car. The airbags had popped up, but she was found far away on the highway. Was she alone?" he asked.

"Yes," I said. "She was supposed to be alone."

The longer we spoke, the more the agony grew from holding in such sorrow and fear. It was growing rapidly every second. I didn't want to accept what I was hearing. I hoped that it was all a mistake and Lisa was sleeping soundly at her friend's house. This couldn't be true. Lisa was a very good driver—better than me. She'd never even had one speeding ticket or any traffic violation. I knew for sure, and from her friends too, that she was always the driver if they went out together and that she would never drink and drive. When I asked the state trooper if alcohol was involved, I was thinking about the other drivers. He told me no, alcohol was not involved, but that they would send her samples to Washington, DC, to test for drugs.

"It will take a couple months to get the results, but when they're ready, we will send them to you."

Now I was angry. "Why not to Boston? Why all the way to Washington, DC?" I asked. He told me that it was now the law with complex accidents.

"Did you check out the other drivers for alcohol and drugs?" I asked.

"We can't tell you that. It isn't your business," he replied.

"It's NOT my business? My daughter was killed!" I screamed.

"No, I can't tell you. It's the law," he replied.

"I want to see my daughter!" I demanded. I turned from the state troopers to the chaplain.

"No, you can't see her," they told me. But I was determined, and they said, "We can't let you see her. Her body is damaged."

The state trooper asked me if I wanted Lisa's stuff back. I knew she kept a lot of stuff in her car. He specifically asked about her new iPod. "Her iPod is broken," he announced. At first, I told him no, I did not want it back, but I quickly changed my mind and asked for everything, even her broken iPod. He told me that we would get her stuff back after they'd finished their investigation. We never did. Of all the stuff that was in her car, we only ever got back her high school yearbook.

The sadness and disbelief I felt were like a physical weight on my shoulders, weighing me down, draining me of life. I was weary and frazzled, but I knew I had to be strong. It felt as if I was in the middle of some nightmare, a dark tornado roaring around me. Everything was moving, and nothing stood still but me. Nothing made sense. No, this couldn't be real.

My sister Jola called.

"Dana," she said. "I heard there was a bad car accident—" I did not let her finish. "It's Lisa's."

"I'm on my way over with my brother-in-law. I'm too nervous to drive myself," she said. For me, it wasn't long before they arrived. The same state trooper repeated exactly what he'd said to me to my sister and her brother-in-law.

The chaplain and state troopers stayed in my house for three hours. They talked with my family. They said that two more cars were involved but ran away, and they talked about this. I stopped listening. It was too much for me to bear.

Finally, the pressure mounting in me broke. I began to sob loudly. I did not care that the police were still there. I was standing like a shrunken statue, feeling the crash, the pain, and the terror of that moment. The police told me that she did not suffer.

I did believe them. I wanted to die too, and I was surprised that I didn't.

"Please, Lord, take me. Let me be killed instead. Let her live," I cried. My body hurt. My stomach was aching.

I wanted to be alone, but the chaplain sent for my son, Peter, and he came with his girlfriend. He lived in a condo about two miles from our home. We cried together. When the police left, more calls came, more people… I did not pay attention anymore. The pastor came with my fellows from my church to pray. I was exhausted.

I knew my life had changed forever.

When everyone finally left, only Peter stayed with me. I was glad to have him close.

We did not talk, but we felt the unity of our sorrow, the warmth of love that allowed us to understand each other without any words. "I will stay with you until Daddy comes back from Australia," Peter said. When the Big Dig had wrapped up in Boston, Ben's engineering company moved him around to projects in many different places. He had recently been assigned a short project in Australia, so on July 15, 2012, that's where he was.

The two of us went upstairs to Lisa's room. It was messy.

"I have to clean up before Ben comes back," I said. I wanted Lisa's room to look like it usually did for him, clean and nice. I also felt as if it was better to do something to stay occupied rather than just sitting and crying.

Peter offered to help me. Every single movement was a forced effort. It felt as if I suddenly weighed one hundred pounds more than usual, and I just wanted to tuck into my bed or hide in some dark corner and die.

As strong as my desire was, I knew I needed to be strong for Peter and Ben. They don't need another death, I reminded myself. I am not alone, and they are suffering just like me. How beautiful it is to have a family to hug and to cry together. We don't have to say a word. We understand each other's pain. I knew that hiding would be much worse. It could bring weakness and even sickness. By the time we finished cleaning her room, it was noon.

"Mom," Peter said anxiously, "I feel that I have to pray for Lisa."

"Okay, Peter," I said. "We will pray in her room."

## Lisa: I'm Okay

It was now about noon of the day of preparation
for the Passover. And Pilate said to the people,
"Here is your king!"

—John 19:14 (NLT)

I had never heard Peter pray before. He'd begun believing in God two years before. His faith did not come easily. At that moment, I sensed it was the right time for him. He prayed with all of the sorrow in his heart. His hands were shaking as he wept and prayed for his sister and for forgiveness of his sins. He had accepted Jesus as his Lord and Savior. A warm feeling of hope and love embraced me then. I was thankful and happy for Peter.

After praying together, Peter and I drove to the nearby Stop & Shop to get some of the necessities. When we stepped out of the car in the parking lot, I suddenly envisioned my Lisa's smiling, happy face in the clouds above us. She was waving to us, saying, "I'm okay. I'm okay."

I hesitated to tell Peter what I'd seen. I looked at him, and he slowed down and stopped. Then before I could say a word, Peter told me about the vision he'd just had.

"Peter," I interrupted him, "how long ago did you see this?"

"Maybe a minute or two ago. I was wondering if I should mention it to you," he said.

"Peter," I said, "we had the same vision at the same time." We embraced in sorrow, and the tears drifted from our eyes.

## Ben: Arrival

The light from the sun was gone. And suddenly,
the thick veil hanging in the temple was torn apart.
Then Jesus shouted, "Father, I entrust my spirit
into your hands!" And with those words
he breathed his last.

—Luke 23:45–46 (NLT)

In Australia, July 15, 2012 was a Monday. When Ben checked his e-mail before work, he was surprised to see a picture of a car accident on the computer screen. Peter sent it to him with this short e-mail:

Daddy, call me. It's important.

Bernard still never wants to talk about what that day was like for him, and I didn't ask too much. It was as if we had been thrown into the midst of war, and yet we were surprised that life around us seemed to be continuing like normal. We lost our beloved and only daughter, and our world felt as if it were crashing down. It took Ben two days to arrive home. When he walked through the door, we didn't say a word to each other, but all three of us embraced for a very long time and cried. We had no idea that this nightmare would only become worse. Two days after the car accident, while we were busy organizing Lisa's funeral and trying to cope with the crushing grief of going on without her, we received calls from family members and friends telling us that on July 17, the accident was in the newspapers and on TV. Reporters had announced that state police believed the teen girl was at fault. "The accident is still under investigation," they said. But they wrote that Lisa had been driving on the wrong side of the highway. The moment we heard the news reports, we were in complete shock. I could not believe that this was happening.

In all of the articles, they wrote that four cars had been involved: Lisa's car, the other victim's GMC pickup truck, a 2002 Chevy Tahoe, and a 2001 Chevy Cavalier. But we knew from speaking with the state troopers who came to our house that morning that two other cars had also been involved—a minivan and a big tractor-trailer that ran over Lisa's car. They suspected that big tractor-trailer hit other cars involved and then ran away from the accident scene. Why hadn't the police told this important detail to the media?

And with the accident still under investigation, why was the media reporting the opposite of what we'd been told by the state police? A million thoughts were racing through my mind. *Was it because they'd heard my accent and felt I'd be easy to take advantage of? Perhaps because they knew my daughter Lisa would never have a chance to argue and tell her side of the story? Who was involved in this car accident? What is being covered up and why?* We were terrified. We tried to call anyone we could, but nobody wanted to talk to us. I called to the state police office. Their officers had been at the scene of the accident, and when I began to ask about the investigation and what had been published, the officer I spoke to was arrogant and rude to me. My voice was shaking on the phone with him, and I could barely get my words out. He did not want to give me any information. Finally, he screamed in my ear, saying, "Don't call back here!" Then he hung up the phone.

We managed to arrange the funeral during this hectic time with help from my son's girlfriend and from fellow members of my church. They prepared everything for us. I did not know how to express how thankful I was. A lot of people showed us compassion, and I was very grateful. They offered their sympathy and helped by bringing us food. I felt like a robot—frozen inside but still completing tasks. If you had pinched me during that time, I'm sure I wouldn't have felt a thing. I did not want to eat. The thought of food disgusted me, so I decided to fast to honor my daughter's departure from this life; it felt right and more calm this way.

Did we still believe in God? Of course we did. We needed Him now more than ever, and we prayed often. Together or separate from each other, we prayed with fellows from church, with Lisa's friends, and with our neighbors who came to pay their respect. We were crying, hugging, and praying. We wanted to be as close to our Lisa as we possibly could be. We spent a lot of time reading the Bible, especially verses about heaven. I wanted to know exactly how big the New Jerusalem from Revelation 21:15–17 (NLT) would be.

We went so far as to look for the answer online, even searching for pictures, when suddenly a book came up in our search—*To Heaven and Back* by Mary C. Neal. It was a memoir about her death, what she saw in heaven, and how she came back to life again.

"That's the book I mentioned to you on the phone!" Ben exclaimed when he saw the picture. "Remember? Before Lisa's accident happened, I told you that when I got home from Australia, we should buy it and read it. I forgot the title, but I recognize the writer's picture on the book cover. I saw her on TV when I was watching *The 700 Club*.

"It's amazing," my husband Ben continued. "I'd completely forgotten about it, and now when we need it and are looking for encouragement, this book appears."

Ben was right. It was amazing. The book is still a great comfort to us. We believe Lisa has met Mary's son, Willy, in heaven. They had incredibly similar demeanors—energetic, positive, and very social. His car accident also happened when he was nineteen, the same age that Lisa was when her accident happened, and in New England, where we live. In her book, Mary mentioned that she had a sign from an owl.

Lisa and I saw an owl a few months before her accident. We never saw owls in the woods before. What's more, in 2011, I put a sign up in my living room with the saying, "Be the change you wish to see in the world." I learned from this book that the quote was Mahatma Gandhi's. Did this book appear to us coincidently? Mary C. Neal wrote that she doesn't believe in coincidences, and neither do I.

## Funeral

O God, listen to my cry! Hear my Prayer!
From the ends of the earth, I will cry to you for
help, for my heart is overwhelmed.
Lead me to the towering rock of safety.

—Psalm 61:1 (NLT)

As part of the final preparations, we met with the funeral director on Wednesday July 18, 2012 at noon, to discuss details. He was surprised that we wanted to know the date and time that our daughter would be cremated. He didn't know, and he told us that it could happen that day in the afternoon, Thursday, or Friday. We explained to him that we wanted to arrive at the crematorium at the exact time it would happen in order to pray for our daughter.

At the end of our meeting with the funeral director, we'd arranged the wake for Sunday and the memorial mass for Monday. He gave us the address and phone number for the cremation house and told us that he would be sending Lisa to the crematory that afternoon, so she was still there if we wanted to pray for her. We went downstairs and prayed at the door of the room she was in. We were not allowed to see her because it had been marked as not to be seen, the funeral director explained to us. As we prayed at the door, I was glued to it, crying and desperately calling her name. "Lisa, Lisa, come back," I begged. I felt such a strong energy coming from the room, and it seemed so helpless and so angry at me for calling her back. I understood that she couldn't return; her body was broken and was not functioning anymore, but it did not stop me from longing for it.

As soon as we arrived back home, a gentle storm began and we held each other, looking through the window at the gray cloudy sky as the quiet thunder and rain rolled in on a delicate breeze. It felt as if Jesus was crying with us, and we felt calmed by it. We did not have to mourn alone. God was mourning with us.

Ben called the cremation house later that same day and left a message. It was important for him to be with Lisa at this last moment. When he didn't hear anything back, he called the next day, Thursday, all morning until noon. Still nobody answered. Before four o'clock that afternoon, Ben became very upset, suddenly anxious.

"Dana, we have to go," he said. "Please hurry. It is happening now! She is calling to me in my head. She is telling me, 'Come, Daddy. I don't want to be alone.' We need to go now!"

In the previous year, when my husband was working overseas, Lisa was always the one who drove him to the airport and said good-bye last. He told me it was always very hard and they always cried even when they promised they would not.

This time Lisa was departing, and we were the ones who needed to say good-bye. I knew it would still just be for a while, temporarily. Eventually, we will be together forever, and we'll never have to say good-bye to each other again.

> "So we are always confident, even though we know
> that as long as we live in those bodies we are not
> at home with the Lord. That is why we live by
> believing and not by seeing."
>
> —2 Corinthians 5:6–7 (NLT)

It was easy to find the place; it wasn't far, and we arrived at ten past four. The cremation house looked nice, like a ranch house. In the bright sunlight, it was almost cheerful. When we tried to enter, it was locked, and we noticed that the two chimneys were already active. My husband and I cried and prayed. It was a beautiful afternoon.

"I know it is the second chimney," I said to Ben. I can't explain how I knew, but I was sure of it.

"Me too," Ben answered. He wanted to stand by that side of the house, but I felt a strong pull to the front, so we stood separate for a while as we prayed. We stayed for the duration. After two hours, we heard the cooling system start.

"It's done," Ben said. "I read the information on their website." We were glad to have made it there for almost the entire process and decided to come back in the morning when they opened just to check in. We spent the rest of the day in Lisa's room and prayed.

It was very hard for us to fall asleep that night. We were plagued by fear, frustration, disappointment, and pain. We spoke about this as a family, and we all admitted to experiencing the same sort of guilt. We all felt as if we should have been better advisors, we should have spent more time with her, we should have protected her from this. Though it was hard, we each resolved not to blame each other and not to run from our own transgressions also. We would pray and ask for forgiveness as many times as we needed, but we would not run from our guilt. We made the effort to find peace with our own guilt, believing if we ask God for forgiveness it will be done; it is one of God's promises.

"But if we confess our sins to Him, He is faithful and just to forgive us and to cleanse us from every wrong" (1 John 1:9, NLT). We were not angry with God. We understood it was not right to think like that.

"Should we accept only good things from the hand of God and never anything bad?" (Job 1 2:10 (NLT).

Jesus Christ was never angry with our Heavenly Father, so why should we be? Many times, as I thought on areas where I had fallen short, God reminded me of the important advice that I'd given to my beloved daughter: always make Jesus the most important person in your life. That same advice was instrumental in helping me cope.

## The First Vision

### Jesus Leading Lisa to His Kingdom

Listen to my prayer, O God.
Do not ignore my cry for help!
—Psalm 55:1 (NLT)

When I finally fell asleep, I had a vision that I was joining a meeting in a very bright place. In the middle of this bright meeting stood a man who was clearly an important leader. As I became more aware and more lucid of my surroundings, I realized I was standing in front of the cremation house, and this man—this leader with bright clothes, beautiful long thick wavy hair and beard, his luminescent face I could not see clearly—was coming out of the cremation house and walking, or rather his walk was like sliding, straight to me and entered into me. Then he walked back, still facing me, to the cremation house and again was coming out, walking toward me. But this time, I noticed Lisa following very closely behind him, so close like he was carrying her on his back. She was staring intensely at him with her eyes wide open, and as the two of them passed me,

I called to her, "Lisa, Lisa," but she did not look at me or even blink. She just continued following this man to the gate of the cemetery.

They were not talking, but I sensed they were still communicating. I noticed Lisa did not seem sad though she was serious, and I knew she was concerned about me.

When I woke up, it was 3:45 a.m. *It was around this time when Lisa's accident happened*, I thought. I walked to Lisa's room, wondering who the man leading her had been. I lied down on Lisa's bed, crying and praying until the sun started to rise. As I was looked around Lisa's room, my eyes came to rest on her painted cross. It had Jesus on it and became more vibrant as daylight broke through the windows. Suddenly, I realized it was Him. It was Jesus. He'd had the same thick wavy hair and beard as the man from Lisa's cross.

Jesus led my Lisa to his kingdom. I was thinking about what I should do, what we all should do. *I have to keep my eyes on Jesus always.* I couldn't wait until Ben woke up to share my vision with him.

After breakfast that morning, we drove again to the crematory house.

This time, the door was unlocked, and a young man was sitting at the desk.

"Can I help you?" he asked.

"Yes, we were here yesterday afternoon, ten after four o'clock, and you were closed," Ben said.

I added, "We were expecting our daughter to be cremated here on either Wednesday, yesterday, or today."

"We called Wednesday afternoon and again yesterday morning, and we left messages on the phone, but nobody answered."

"I'm sorry," the young man said. "The owners are on vacation. They will be back after tomorrow. I'm alone now and very busy, mostly downstairs where the furnaces are, and we don't have a phone there."

"We were here yesterday at ten past four," I began.

We explained to him what happened, that yesterday before four o'clock, Lisa was calling her dad to say good-bye.

"Yesterday?" the young man asked. He turned on his computer. "I can check. Yes, I started just ten minutes before four o'clock yesterday." He was excited and amazed. "You have to come back when the owner returns from vacation and tell him!" he said. We promised him that we would and felt uplifted as we left. When we returned and told the owner the full story, he took us downstairs and asked us which chimney we had stood near. "You said the second chimney?" he asked. "Which one? Depending which side you look from, it could be one, two"—he pointed—"or two, one."

"This one," I said, pointing before he'd even finished. He was so amazed that he took me to the cemetery and said, "Choose any place you want for your cross." I chose to place it in front of the crematorium, near the spot where, in my vision, I'd seen Jesus lead Lisa.

The wake was that Sunday in the funeral home with the pastor who'd baptized Lisa and me, and the memorial mass was the next day at our church. A lot of people came, and they brought us flowers and cards. Even at this very difficult moment, we witnessed God's love for us. At the funeral, one couple was very anxious to share a story with us. The woman said, "Our daughter, Carolyn, called my cell phone to tell us that her good friend Lisa had passed away earlier that morning. She was very upset, and we told her how sorry we were for her. Within a minute of the phone call, we were driving down Franklin Street, and there was a rainbow in one of the few clouds in the sky. We couldn't believe it because it hadn't rained at all and was sunny nice weather. As we got closer to our home, we noticed that the rainbow was right in the area over your house. We knew, we said. 'It's right over Lisa's parents' house.' We had never seen anything like it before."

I asked her what time it had happened, and she said it was around 11:45 a.m. It was the same time as when our son, Peter, had been praying with me for Lisa and accepted Jesus into his heart as his Lord and Savior.

> "The message is close at hand; it is on your lips and
> in your heart. For if you confess with your mouth
> that Jesus is Lord and believe in your heart that
> GOD raised Him from the dead,
> you will be saved."
>
> —Romans 10:8–9 (NLT)

## The Second Vision

## Shopping with My Daughter

> O God, listen to my prayer.
> Pay attention to my plea.
>
> —Psalm 54:2 (NLT)

The first few days after the funeral, I felt very deeply depressed. It was still difficult to accept what had happened; reality was cruel and struck me with its mighty power. We put Lisa's remains in her room.

On our porch, on the side where Lisa's room is, we had a pot of beautiful exotic red flowers. The red reminded me of the dress Lisa was wearing when I last saw her. Usually, one or two of the flowers blossomed and closed at the evening and then died. This summer, we had a lot of flowers; each day, more showed until they bloomed all at once—nineteen in one day. We needed those signs from her.

We prayed and asked God for more of them. We needed to feel as if we still had some connection with her.

"God blesses those who mourn, for they will be comforted" (Matt. 5:4, NLT).

It was September 13, 2012. I did not dream of anything but heard a voice in my head loudly repeating the words, "You need to accept what happened and be happy that she is in heaven. You need to accept what happened and be happy that she is in heaven…" The voice kept repeating this. It was so jarring that, eventually, it startled me awake. And still, these same words were repeated three more times, deafeningly loud. I was so startled that I jumped from bed and bumped into the wall. In the darkness, I tried to find a pencil and paper to write down what I'd heard so that I wouldn't forget it in the morning. By the time I found something to write with, I was wide awake.

"What happened?" Ben said in a panic.

"Shh…Nothing. Sleep. I will tell you later," I said.

It was well before four in the morning. At that time, the stress in which we were living gripped us so strong that we desperately needed rest, so I wasn't too content with how steadfast God's discipline was, but I was very thankful for the message nonetheless. I understood that He wanted me to shake myself together.

A short while later, I had another vision in a dream with Lisa. During summer vacation, before the accident, she was too busy with her boyfriend and her friends, so I was looking forward to spending some time together with her. The Sunday of the accident, Lisa and I had been planning to go shopping together after she got home from her friend's house. In my vision, I was shopping with Lisa, and she looked so beautiful. It was as if the sun was always shining on her; her skin was sleek and smooth. I had never seen her so happy and energetic. I could not see clearly the man who followed her, but he was with her all the time, very close, everywhere. I asked her, "Who is this man? Is he your boyfriend?"

"No, he's not my boyfriend. He is better than any boyfriend! He is better than anybody! Anything!" she said, laughing. When we came back home, he did not enter our house but waited for her at the door outside. Lisa and I changed into slippers, and I noticed that they were the same size and they fit us both even though Lisa wore a nine and a half and I wear a size six. Now we had the same size and the same-looking slippers, only the tops had different patterns painted on them. We laughed and hugged, and I felt her warm touch. I smelled her. Every one of my senses was full of her love. It was real.

I woke up just before four again, and I thanked the Lord for His mercy and grace. I knew it was Jesus with my daughter, and He is better than anybody and anything! I could still hear Lisa saying this, and I couldn't wait to be with our Lord too. I wondered about the slippers and what it meant that they were miraculously the same size. Perhaps it meant that we have the same size "footprints" in the eyes of God—that we all do. He loves us the same though we are different from each other.

# The Third Vision

## Lisa's Good-Bye

I lift my eyes to you, O God, enthroned in heaven.

—Psalm 123:1 (NLT)

Shortly after this vision with the slippers, I had another vision in a dream. In this vision, I left my bedroom in the morning and went to go to the bathroom to take a bath, but then I saw Lisa in her room. The window was open, the fresh air was gently playing with the light yellow curtain, and Lisa was radiantly beautiful. As she was standing in the sunlight, it was as if happiness and vital energy were exploding inside of her—she looked beautiful and powerful. This time, she was alone. She stood at the open closet door just as she would every morning when choosing what to wear. She was in her black-and-white dress.

This time, I was fully aware that she'd passed away, and I was extremely happy to see her. "Lisa!" I yelled. "You are here!" She came to me, and I felt that she wanted to say good-bye; sadness overwhelmed me. But she wasn't sad. The radiant happiness never left her for a second. She hugged me, and again I could feel her touch, smell her, and embrace her warmth and love. "Can you come again?" I asked her. She looked straight into my eyes and said, "I will be visiting you for the rest of your life."

"Wait," I said. "Wait. I will be back. I'm going for Daddy." I was so happy to see her that I wanted to share it with my husband. I went to our bedroom and woke Ben up.

"Come on! Hurry! Lisa is here!" I said. "You know she passed away, but she is alive! Come on fast!"

"I know she passed away," Ben said. When we came out from our bedroom, she was not there. Only her dress was left on the floor, as if she had slipped out of it and disappeared. I woke up again at the same time, just before four in the morning; but this time, God gave me a promise, that she will be visiting me for the rest of my life. And she is.

"All praise to the God, the Father of our Lord Jesus Christ. He is the source of every mercy and the God who comforts us. He comforts us in all our troubles so that we can comfort others" (2 Cor. 1:3–4, NLT).

I understand the message from this vision. Even now, I still have Lisa's clothes and laundry in her closet to hug and smell. I am struggling to give them away. She wanted me to know that she doesn't need them anymore. Even the dress that she was wearing she left on the floor.

# The Case

## The Last Conversation

The last time I spoke with my beloved daughter Lisa, it was Saturday evening around nine o'clock, just as she was leaving to go to her friend's house. She was wearing her new red dress and looked beautiful. I asked her if she had enough money for gas, and she said she did.

"Will you be home tonight?" I asked.

"I will be back," she said. "I love you."

"I love you," I replied.

It's our family habit that if we depart anytime and anywhere from each other, we are to say "I love you" to each other. It was Lisa who started this in middle school. I had no idea what a gift this habit would be to me now.

## The Cross

Lisa's boyfriend Eric and Eric's father made a cross for her. They told me that they repainted it a few times until they felt that Lisa would be happy with it. The final time they repainted this cross, they were listening to the radio and "If I Die Young" by the Band Perry began to play. They knew then that the painting was finally right. I do think it expresses her bright, positive outlook, especially the pink hearts. They wanted to put this cross on the highway where the accident happened, but I believed that God had a different plan. We put this cross close to the site of my first vision of Lisa—near the cemetery exit where Jesus led her out to his kingdom.

Before Lisa's accident, I was not happy that she and Eric were dating. He was four years older than Lisa and lived with a few other boys in a rental house in Bridgewater, where they often had all-night parties. She frequently stayed with him in this house, and I did not like it at all. Lisa believed in him though. She told me that I didn't know him, that he is a smart and hardworking boy. I knew she cared for him, but like most mothers, I was concerned and worried. My last conversation with both Eric and Lisa together was the day before this tragic night. Lisa was arguing with him about something in the kitchen, and when I came in, she said, "Mom, he is forcing me to drive late at night to see him!" I could not help but react in anger. As a mother, my instinct was to protect Lisa at all costs, so I immediately confronted him.

"Why would you do that? Don't you know how dangerous it is? Don't you know how many trucks are driving like crazy at that time of night?"

When he didn't respond, I turned to Lisa and said, "Don't do it! You don't have to listen to him!" She started to march upstairs to her room, but I did not let it go that easily. "If he loves you, he would not do this!" I called after her in frustration. I was worried for her and hoped she would not listen to him. I knew from talking to Lisa that Eric worked hard to save money for school, took some college classes, and was disciplined about going to the gym regularly, but I still wasn't sure that he could take care of my daughter. Lisa's friend Joni, whose house in Providence Lisa was at that night before the accident, told me that Eric and Lisa had been arguing on the phone and that Eric wanted her to come to his house. Lisa decided to go to his house before coming home, but she never made it home. Eric told the state police and me that he wasn't home. He was with his friends and planned to return before Lisa got there, but he didn't. It had happened in the past; Lisa would stop at Eric's house in Bridgewater on the way home from her friend's house in Providence. Sometimes, she changed her mind though and would bypass Exit 15 on the highway to, instead, drive straight home.

After Lisa's accident, Peter, who didn't know about the last conversation I had with Eric and Lisa, was surprised when Eric said to him, "Your mother probably hates me!" Peter asked me what he meant by that, and I told him about the last conversation we'd had. But I did not hate Eric. I can't; Lisa loved him. My family and I were in so much pain that we didn't have room for any other negative feelings. I was surprised to discover the depth of my own strength during this trying time. My family banded together to support each other, showing kindness and helping each other when we needed it. We were alert and faced each day like warriors. I don't believe that we did this on our own; God was at work in our lives and carried us when we could not stand. Though I have deep regrets about this last day, I do not hate Eric. I was not even angry with him. How could he have known this would happen? He was completely devastated when he found out. We all were trapped by darkness.

After Lisa's funeral, I met with Eric at my house, and I told him about my first vision with Lisa. He told me that he'd had some visions too. I brought Eric to Lisa's room and gave him the Bible I had bought for him. We prayed and cried, and I asked him if he wanted to accept Jesus as his Lord and Savior. He was not sure. I didn't know if he did this because he was sorry for me and I asked him to or if he really needed it from his heart, but I'm sure Lisa would be happy that I took the opportunity to reach out to him. I decided to pray for him more often and to get to know him better.

## Everything Changes

O God: guide my steps by your word, so I will not
be overcome by any evil

—Psalm 119:133 (NLT)

Even before we started to arrange a funeral for Lisa, we began receiving letters from lawyers representing people involved in this car accident. It seemed cruel and aggressive to me, and incredibly disrespectful. I wondered what the hurry was. How hard would it have been for them to wait a few days until at least after the funeral?

We knew we needed a lawyer too. My husband, Ben, decided to find some work closer to our home and not go back to Australia. It was a very tough but necessary decision; we needed to stay close to each other. We felt as if we were attacked from every direction. We put our trust and hope in God. We felt tremendously overwhelmed by the fear, stress, and grief, which continued to weigh on us. We were praying more and making every effort to be sensitive to each other and be incredibly loving and kind.

Ben tried to contact the state police who had been on the accident scene, but to no avail. No one was available. Ben was informed that the state trooper who was at the accident scene, who arrived at my door with the news, now was reassigned to a different division and was not working there anymore. When he had no luck finding someone there who was willing to talk to him, he kept digging and found the number for the State Police Collision Analysis & Reconstruction Section on Google.

Ben called them and spoke to the lieutenant who was in charge and investigating the case. He admitted to Ben that there had been another car involved in this accident, which ran away from the scene. He also stated repeatedly that no charges would be filed against Lisa. After they discussed the accident, the lieutenant mentioned that he thought Lisa must have gotten confused and driven the wrong way on the road. He said that detectives from the District Attorney's Office were investigating this case and that an officer from the reconstruction team, who worked for him, had some physical evidence to suggest this, such as some tire skids they thought proved she was driving the wrong way. But with six cars involved and many others running through the accident scene before the police came and could stop traffic, there were certainly many crisscrossing tire skids. Later, we learned in the first report that most of the skids burned away long before the investigation team could arrive on the scene because the pickup truck involved was on fire and likely most of the tire skids were washed away by the fire truck too. After his conversation with the lieutenant in charge, Ben tried to contact the reconstruction officer, but he was on vacation; and after that, he had a very busy schedule, so Ben could not meet with him right away.

## The Sign

I will cause wonders in the heavens and on the earth.

—Joel 2:30 (NLT)

After Ben came back from Australia, it was a very crazy time for my family emotionally, physically, and financially. All the circumstances that we had to face were crazy. It was like being at the front lines in a battle and watching out to not step on a mine. Ben lost his job. Lisa was inequitably blamed for the car accident, and her car was registered in my name. The future was a big question mark. How would we handle this? And how would we live our lives now without our beloved only daughter, Lisa?

My son got a lawyer for us, but from the very beginning, something about him didn't sit right with me. He told us to wait, so we waited. He told us that, first, we should let our car insurance take care of this case, that they have their own lawyers to defend and fight for us. It sounded right, so we sent all the information we had to our car insurance too. Our lawyer promised to lead the case, and he gave us his phone numbers and e-mail address, but he barely answered any of our calls. He just kept telling us that we should wait. The lack of communication from him was frustrating. I wanted to get a new lawyer, but I didn't know what to do or how to find the right attorney for our case. It was exhausting. How long would this nightmare continue?

The second night Ben was home from Australia, before we prayed in the evening in Lisa's room, Ben and I were completely worn down. Sitting on Lisa's bed, we cried. With Ben on my right side, we began praying. I prayed earnestly, asking God for help and to be our lawyer.

As we prayed, I suddenly felt somebody begin to tickle my left arm and side. The tickling was unmistakable, and it increased to the point that it almost hurt. At first, I couldn't help but laugh out loud, but as fear overwhelmed my surprise, I said, "Stop. You're hurting me!" I knew it was Lisa. Only she would do something like that. My husband looked at me with fear and surprise. I could only imagine what he was thinking. When I explained to him what had happened, he was very happy. For the remainder of the time we spent praying, Lisa remained on my left arm; but this time, she was very gentle. To this day, I sometimes still feel Lisa's hand on my left arm. People have asked me, "Why the left arm?" and "How are you sure that it's Lisa?" Whenever we were together, I liked to have her on my left side—my heart side, I told her. And Lisa almost always had very cold hands, and this hand is sometimes cold.

I was very grateful to God for this wonderful sign. It is definitely helping me and my family in very painful moments when we desperately miss Lisa.

Every morning, I spend a long time on prayer and meditation. We pray to God for justice, asking for His mercy, protection, and loving guidance. From the start, I believed with all my heart, and I know from God that Lisa had not been driving on the wrong side of the highway that night. I felt that I needed to vindicate her name. I spoke to Joni, Lisa's girl friend with whom she spent this last night of her life, and she told me confidently, repeating a few times in disbelief, "Mrs. Banat, Lisa was not drinking. I know." I said, "But my duty is to ask you." They had been at home watching a movie. This car accident was not Lisa's fault. She was just driving home as she'd promised and had been about a mile from Exit 17, which she would have taken to get home, when the accident happened. I asked Joni what time it was when Lisa left her to go home. She told me that maybe was about 2:15 a.m. She wasn't sure about the exact time. From Joni's to Lisa's home is about one hour and fifteen minutes, depending on the traffic, and not an easy drive. Ben and I traced Lisa's course from Joni's to our home. Later we noticed that in the State Police report, it states that the time of accident was 3:45 a.m. That estimate seems off by about fifteen minutes. It could be that she drove to her boyfriend's home in Bridgewater, which was not so far from Route 24, and because he wasn't home, she immediately drove back to Exit 15 on Route 24, and then, about one mile further, had the accident. It could be that Joni's time was inaccurate.

I had a clear message from the Lord that I had to go to the public with this case, but I didn't know how to do that. I couldn't do it by myself because I did not like using computers and now I needed one.

Lisa used to help me with every computer task I needed to do, but now I would need to learn for myself. My husband was too busy looking for new jobs and trying to find out more information about the car accident. He tried to contact anyone who was assigned to this case. We still hadn't had any contact with the reconstruction team. Ben requested to at least see our daughter's car after the crash—it had been towed to a place nearby in Brockton—but he was told that it would not be possible until after the investigation was completed. We were never granted permission.

"Ben, we have to go to the media with this. The TV news or newspapers maybe. God wants me to go to the public," I announced.

Ben was surprised. "We don't know what evidence they have," he answered.

"Nothing!" I said. "We shouldn't be afraid. I know that Lisa is innocent and that she was not driving the wrong way. We have to trust the Lord."

"Wait a little," Ben said.

"We shouldn't wait, Ben," I argued. But I knew I would not get far without my family's help and I couldn't count on them now with this issue. Doubt and fear paralyzed them. I had no choice. I had to learn to use the computer fast.

## Meeting with the officer who led the reconstruction

But Peter and the apostle replied, "We must obey God rather than human authority."

—Acts 5:29 (NLT)

On August 22, 2012, almost six weeks after the car accident, we had a scheduled meeting. We were nervous to meet with the reconstruction officer. The evening before our meeting, I prayed to God with a heavy heart.

"Lord," I asked. "Please give me some information about this officer, so that he will know that you are on our side. Is he a Christian?"

"Yes," I heard in my head.

"Does he have children?" I asked.

"Yes," I heard.

"How many?"

"Two," I heard.

"A boy and a girl?"

"Two boys," I heard.

"What should I say to him? How will he know that you are on our side?"

"Ask him, 'Are you still married?'"

It was frightening to me to ask him this question. I don't know him. It's not my business how he is doing with his marriage. I expected from God something different. So I was thinking about how to ask the officer this question. As soon as we met with him, he asked, "How much do you know?" He seemed agitated. "How much do you know?" he repeated aggressively.

I interrupted. "Are you Christian?"

"Yes," he answered.

I was not brave enough to ask him if he was still married, so instead, I asked simply, "Are you married?"

"Yes," he said slowly. He seemed suspicious and surprised.

"And you have two children. Two boys," I said.

"How do you know?" he asked me.

"I was praying for you, and God told me," I answered.

"That's amazing. Really, it's amazing" he said, and he shook his head.

"Yes, God is amazing," I said. "Can we pray together?"

"Yes," he replied. I prayed for justice and truth. It was something I'd never done before or ever expected to do—praying in a state police office with a state trooper. Later, I was not at peace with our conversation, so I e-mailed him to say that God wanted me to ask him, "Are you still married?" and I am prying for him. He never e-mailed me back.

But after we prayed with the officer, Ben put a map on the table and showed him how Lisa was driving from

Providence to her boyfriend's in Bridgewater and then
to her home in Mansfield. He explained to him how
improbable it was for her to get confused since she knew
the area by heart. The year before, Lisa was always visiting
her friend in Providence, and she was very familiar with the
route. She was attending college in this exact area as well.

## Map

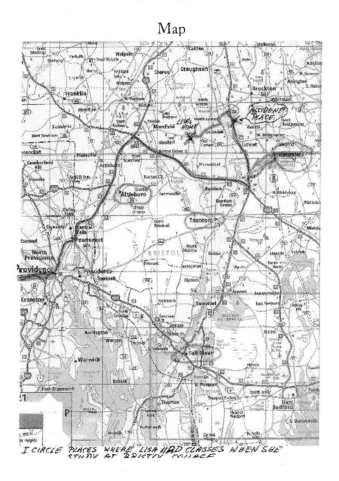

I CIRCLE PLACES WHERE LISA HAD CLASSES WHEN SHE
STUDY AT BRISTOL COLLEGE

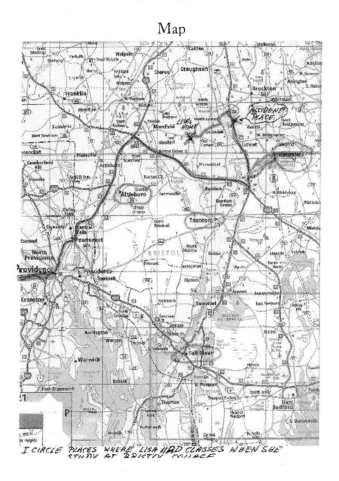71

Lisa was a very responsible driver and a good student. She had a completely clean driving record, no speeding tickets or violations of any kind. She loved driving, and she was very good at it. She was always the designated driver whenever she went out with her friends. During her last two years, she drove about 75,000 miles, driving mostly to work and to school in Fall River, Bridgewater, and Attleboro. She knew that area incredibly well because it was part of her routine to drive through there almost every day. The officer was also very surprised that we knew about the two other cars that had ran away. He wanted to know who gave us this information and how much more we knew. He did not want to include the minivan or the big tractor trailer in the report of the car accident scene. When I told him that we had this information from his boss, the lieutenant in charge, he admitted—that yes, they were involved. He then drew a sketch explaining how the accident had happened, starting to describe the reconstruction by immediately assuming that Lisa was driving the wrong way and hit the pickup truck head-on and to its left side. He did not even consider other scenarios. We later learned from the first report that the woman from the pickup truck who survived this accident said she was awake the whole time and did not see Lisa's car or her headlights in front of her car; in fact, she did not see any car. The officer explained that after the initial impact, the momentum caused Lisa's car to roll over, bounce off of the concrete Jersey barrier, and land in the middle lane of the road, as shown on the newspaper photos.

Because of the momentum after the impact, the pickup truck would've had to have made a 360-degree turn and then an additional 90-degree turn to land perpendicular to the roadway ahead of Lisa's car as it had. Much can be gained by looking at the position of the cars shown in the newspaper photos of the accident scene. This scenario seems very unlikely. The reconstruction officer told my husband that he could show him all his calculations and measurements, but he never did. The reconstruction did not even include the role of the tractor trailer or the Tahoe, which was also shown in the newspaper photos standing in front of Lisa's car and the three other cars involved, with heavy damages to its front.

"I cannot understand how we can even talk about an accurate reconstruction of this accident and not include all of the vehicles involved," Ben said. "To calculate how far and in what positions the cars would land after the collision, we have to know the exact speeds of both cars at the time of collision and the angles they hit each other at. Otherwise, all the theoretical calculations cannot be accurately performed," Ben continued. "Just before colliding, the cars would more than likely have tried to slow down or at least have made some side turns to avoid each other."

But the reconstruction officer did not want to include the big tractor trailer in this scenario. He pointed to the evidence of the skid marks, which he had. For us, it was very doubtful evidence. Later, from the first report, we learned that a lot of cars went through the accident scene before police stopped the traffic, and the reconstruction team arrived around thirty or forty minutes after that.

Ben pointed out that the skid marks in the newspaper photos, when magnified, pointed to a completely different scenario and a different sequence of events just before this crash that would also need to be considered. Ben had worked for fourteen years as commissioning engineer of the main transportation control center in the Boston area.

During his career, he witnessed and was involved in the reconstruction of numerous traffic accidents by analyzing different scenarios, photographs, and video records from various car accidents and crashes that happened on the Central Artery, in tunnels, and on the highway. The officer promised that he would discuss the report and consult with Ben before the second and final report was issued, but he never did.

We asked to see the footage from the cameras that were installed above the highway where this accident occurred, but the officer was not sure if they worked.

"What does that mean?" I asked. "You are not sure? Did you check?" He was silent.

I told him that I would do everything I could to know the truth, even if I had to go to the public or appeal to the president. I felt tenseness growing, and I changed the subject, talking about how hard it is for marriages to go through sorrow like that. He said that he'd seen similar tragedies really negatively affect some couples. From his experience, most of the people he'd seen in these situations usually got divorced within two years. He'd seen a similar situation with his relatives, he told us.

"Not us," I promise. "We have faith and that makes a difference."

"I see that," he said.

Through all the difficult circumstances we'd gone through together in the past, we supported each other. Now God supported us. We were both hurt, scared, and weak. We had to completely rely on God.

We were very disappointed after our meeting with the reconstruction officer. Route 24 is a very popular and busy highway close to Boston, and there are cameras installed in this area. I suspect that the cameras would have registered the car driving the wrong way as well as the van and tractor trailer. Somebody must have seen this tractor trailer after it left the scene. It would have had visible damages after crashing through my daughter's car and others.

We didn't understand why the officer did not want to include the Tahoe in this car accident reconstruction despite it being in the newspaper photos of the scene. It was only after a long argument that he admitted the Tahoe was even involved. He claimed that it had only been hit by the tractor trailer and he did not want to tell us who was driving this car. Later, we found out that the man was a resident of Brooklyn, New York, who had been driving without a license. We also discovered that the car he was driving was not his and there was a police warrant for him from Fall River. At the end of this meeting, he told us that he only had responsibility for a small portion of this investigation and that the detectives from the district attorney's office were leading this case.

## The Tunnel

I wait quietly before God, for my hope is in him.

—Psalm 62:5 (NLT)

There was a very depressing atmosphere in our home. Ben was still trying to find a job closer to home. A man who claimed he could help Ben was not answering his e-mails, and later, we found out that he was in the hospital expecting surgery.

"Ben," I said, "we have to pray for him and for a miracle." So we prayed. We reminded God that we trusted Him with our future when we prayed in the chapel in Germany as immigrants and that we're so thankful for the many blessings He had provided us. Bernard was never without work after we immigrated to Canada and then the USA. We still trusted God with our future and needed to be patient. We waited for the answer to our prayers.

A few days later, the man who'd been helping Ben to find a job called him from the hospital. He was happy and optimistic that it wasn't a serious heart problem, which the doctors had suspected. It appeared to be just an inflamed gallbladder, and he would soon be back to work. In the meantime, he said he was still in the hospital just sitting in bed with his laptop on his knees, looking for work for my husband. The closest assignment he was able to find was in Canada.

We were overwhelmingly thankful for this man's recovery and for Ben's new job. We gave thanks to God for answering our prayers. It would take some time to get a work visa and medical exam and to make other preparations, but at least we'd have more time together. I had to remain in our home to take care of Lisa's case.

We knew that we would be apart again, and I did not like to think about it. I focused on just embracing every moment I spent with Ben. We often went to La Salette Shrine in Attleboro. It is a very peaceful, relaxing place surrounded by a grove, woods, and a small lake. We would listen from the grounds to the calming, pleasant Christian music played through the loudspeakers.

In the chapel, we lit candles, prayed, and cried. We never thought that we would have to do this for our own child. It is still shocking to us. Walking around the lake, I remembered how I told my childhood story to Lisa there. Her favorite story was about the tunnel.

It happened around the time when I was in preschool, before I was taken to the orphanage. I was very sick, lying in a crib that was much too small for me, and crying loudly. To this day, I remember how sick I was. My head was burning, and my throat was so dry that it ached. I could not handle it any longer. I had to drink water. I was very scared but so thirsty that I called out for water.

"I want water," I cried. My mother was passed out, drunk; the man who was with her yelled at me. "If you say one more thing, I will punch you in the head!" he threatened. I was sure he would do it too. He scared me. I was afraid that I would die either from this man who would kill me or from this fever, but I was quiet. I wasn't sure what happened next—if I had fallen asleep or passed away—but I was in a cloudy, amber tunnel. I felt surrounded by warmth and love, and suddenly, everything was calm, and I felt safe. But I also felt that I was alone here, and I knew I shouldn't be. In the distance, at the end of this tunnel, was a bright light, and I wanted to go to this light, but whenever I got close, the light got farther away. I tried repeatedly to reach it without any success. Finally, I heard a voice.

"You have to go back," it said. I did not see anybody, but there the voice was again. "You will come back."

I begged the voice, "I don't want go back. I want to stay!"

"You will be back," the voice promised. I woke up in the morning completely healthy—no fever. I wasn't even thirsty. Often after telling her this story, Lisa would remind me that my tunnel wouldn't be empty anymore because now I have a family. For sure, she is waiting for me with Jesus. Now I think it was Jesus's voice that I heard in the amber tunnel.

## "To My Only Daughter"

I've often said, "You are my flower."
In it is beauty and power:
as rose blossoms happy, sweet,

The love becomes her trusty need.

You are like cheerful gentle ring,
You are flourishing like the spring,
Where each color has a warm kiss
From busily humming bees.

When my rose enjoys sheer sun,
Every drop of my tears had run
To the maturing hope which is good
In God's promises, the root of truth.

My Rose grows in my dreams,
In God's garden, with fresh streams,
Her arms are open to me,
At the sacred forever, forever, tree.

Home sweet home forever
With our Father in heaven.

# Facing the Giants

"NOTHING CAN SEPARATE US FROM GOD'S LOVE" What can we say about such wonderful things as these? If God is for us, who can ever be against us? Since God did not spare even His own Son but gave Him up for us all, won't God, who gave us Christ, also give us everything else? Who dares accuse us whom God has chosen for his own? Will God? No! He is the one who has given us right standing with Himself. Who then will condemn us? Will Christ Jesus? No, for He is the one who died for us and was raised to life for us and is sitting at the place of highest honor next to God, pleading for us."

—Romans 8:31–34 (NLT)

Thank you, Heavenly Father, that the followers of Christ can be sure of that! What a wonderful promise that is available to everyone who makes the decision to believe in Jesus Christ and follow him. Our Heavenly Father forgives, comforts, and blesses us in the name of Jesus Christ, our Savior and Redeemer. Amen.

## Meeting with Detectives

After some time passed, whenever I told relatives, friends, or neighbors what we were going through, it seemed as if they had just stopped listening. They didn't want to be bothered by all the contradicting important details that did not add up in the media's story. They would rather ignore the truth.

Facing the giant—that's what seemed to have happened. We are emotional victims of this tragic accident.

Meanwhile, people were watching us, and we sensed the pressure everywhere, even at work and in church. We chose to place our only hope in God.

On August 29, 2012, Ben arranged a meeting with the lead detective and his supervisor from the District Attorney's Office, both who were investigating this accident. As the reconstruction officer had mentioned, they were leading this case.

The meeting was in our home after lunch time. When I was praying for this meeting, I had a warning and was "instructed" not to ask private questions. They knew what happened with the reconstruction officer. But God gave me some information about them, and I tried to warn my family, but they ignored my notice and hoped that the detectives would help us find out the truth.

When we met them, a strange thing happened. Immediately, I knew very strongly that I'd met the lead detective recently.

"I know you," I said. "We met recently. I'm not sure where, but I am positive that we've met."

"No, we didn't meet," he said.

"Are you sure?" I asked. Then it dawned on me. "Did you come to Lisa's wake?"

"No," he replied immediately.

I was not at peace with his answer. Something did not sit right.

"I know we've met. I have to think about it, but it will come to my mind," I said.

When I did not drop it, he finally admitted where we had met.

"Yes, I was at your daughter's wake," he said.

There were hundreds of people at Lisa's wake. A lot of people I didn't know from her high school: teachers, parents, a lot of teenagers. I figured some curious people came too, but I only remembered him. I really didn't recall the others, but he was a stranger who stuck out in my mind.

During Lisa's wake, I retreated inside myself; I was there physically only. I did not pay too much attention to people, but when I saw him, I knew he didn't belong there. Later, after the funeral, the funeral director admitted to us that "they" sometimes came to see what kind of people attended the wakes.

For me, it seemed wrong for them to do that without my husband's and my permission, but at this time, everything was going too quickly, so I did not press the issue.

As we sat down in our living room to talk, the atmosphere was very tense. I did not feel comfortable praying with them, so I asked the detective if he was a Christian, and with a distinct voice, he answered, "Yes." But his boss replied, "I am not."

"Can we pray together?" I asked. We always pray, especially when it's a very important meeting.

Not waiting for an answer, I prayed. The uncomfortable feeling did not leave me and the rest of my family. We all were very tense. It was my husband who started the conversation. He tried to persuade the officers that it wasn't possible that Lisa got confused and drove the wrong way on the highway; it just didn't make any sense.

"She was about one mile before Exit 17, which she would have taken to get home."

"We have witnesses," one of the detectives said. "We got a lot of calls."

"No, you didn't," I said with confidence. "The state trooper who first came to my house on July 15$^{th}$ told me that there were no witnesses, no calls. It was a Sunday night, around 3:40 a.m. It was pitch black, and everything happened very fast."

The boss asked me, "What else do you know?"

I did not understand. Was there more to know? I was surprised that he asked me the same question as the reconstruction officer from collision reconstruction had also asked. Later, I suspected why. The immense stress that my family was under at that time kept us from remembering and mentioning all the details of what the state trooper who first came to my house had told us. After our meeting with the detective, it hit me. On July 15, the state trooper at my door told me that they had been chasing a bad guy at the time that this accident happened and they suspected that he ran from them in the opposite direction on the highway and caused this accident. It seemed to me that the reconstruction officer, then the detective, and his boss were all checking my memory. And at the time, when these two detectives from the Attorney's Office were in our house, my memory was clouded with pain and sorrow, so I did not mention this important detail.

"That's it? That's what you know?" the detective continued. I noticed that the two of them looked at each other.

"Yes," I said with confusion.

The detective mentioned then that they'd found a rope in Lisa's car and they thought that she could have had some problems and asked if we had noticed any strange behavior.

"Are you trying to suggest that she planned a suicide?" I interrupted him. "Nobody who knows Lisa would ever believe you! Nobody!"

"You don't trust us?" the boss asked me. I looked straight into his eyes and clearly told him, "No." I explained that the rope was from Lisa's boyfriend, who worked at a landscaping company and was without a driver's license at that time, so Lisa was driving him to work. I had seen that rope in her car before too and many others tools.

"God knows the truth. Our daughter is innocent," I reminded them. "And the truth will come out."

"We can't talk with her," they said.

My family was not pleased with me either. My husband tried to continue discussing the accident with them. He told them his theory of how it probably happened.

Before our meeting with these detectives, I asked Ben to tell them about his dream, which we believed was the sign from God that we had prayed for. Ben suggested to the detectives that all the cars involved in this accident would have been braking to avoid the car they saw fast approaching from the opposite direction. They may have swerved, bumped into the Jersey barrier or other cars, and spun. Because both safe air bags, the ones at the front and at the side doors popped up, this could save Lisa and she may have walked out of her car then, and at that moment, may have been hit and killed by the tractor trailer that ran through her car and others. This would explain why and how her body had gotten so far away from her car. The boss detective shook his head and said, "No, it wasn't that. We have a thousand calls! The reconstruction officer has some physical evidence, like tire skids going the wrong way." Then the detective suddenly stood up and asked my son to speak with him outside, so they went outside of the house so that nobody would hear them. I went after them to the bathroom and overheard them.

After my husband's long discussion with both detectives about the reconstruction of this accident, they told us that nothing is 100 percent sure. The detectives said they were waiting for the final report from the reconstruction office before they could finalize their report. "They are 'our people,'" the lead detective's boss said. They also said that the investigation was still pending and they could not release any details at that time. However, just as we were finishing our meeting and the detectives were about to leave, the boss alluded to some preliminary findings from a medical analysis that showed a lot of alcohol in her system. They told us they had other special evidence that suggested she was driving the wrong way but that they couldn't release it to us yet. We were puzzled. What does that mean? Did they get Lisa's medical report from Washington DC though we still hadn't heard anything about this? What was the other evidence they had?

It's not possible to describe how painful and disheartening this information was to us. I suspected that something wasn't right. I questioned myself, *What is going on?* We already lived with deep distress, and this information just added another heavy load.

For a while, Peter did not tell us what he'd spoken about with the detective when they went outside our house because he told Peter to keep it secret. But eventually, we convinced Peter that I'd overheard them and we should overcome the fear through faith and not let it control us. The detective had told Peter that they had a "black box" from Lisa's car that could prove that she was driving the wrong way and that they had a preliminary medical report that wasn't good. My husband and I decided to investigate this information that the detective had given Peter. So we went to the Toyota dealership where we'd bought Lisa's car from. They informed us that our daughter's car, a 2010 Toyota Corolla, did not have any black box. Under the dashboard of her car was an electronic chip that, when it is in good condition, can register only the last moment of the car's speed when it crashes, but nothing else.

They informed us that they planned, in the future, for 2015 models to have black boxes available for customers who wanted them, but at the time, it was under negotiation whether or not to put them on the market.

We were very surprised to hear this. I asked, "Can the electronic chip from my daughter's car, a 2010 Corolla, register if someone does a U-turn or what direction they were traveling in?"

"No," the man who was helping us answered. "Only how fast the car was going when it crashed, and that's only if the electronic chip is not damaged or burnt up in the crash."

As we drove back home from the Toyota dealership, we did not talk much. We tried to understand what was going on.

In the movie *Facing the Giants*, the pastor describes losing a child as being like living with an amputation. They both require a process to learn how to live again. But I think losing a child is much more difficult than an amputation because it is not visible. What would I give for my child to still be alive? Everything.

That's how much it hurt. The pain was nearly unbearable. But we were focused on God and stayed strong in our faith. I trusted God, and I did believe Him instead of what these detectives told us. We kept praying and encouraging each other. I was wondering what it meant when God told me to go to the public. At that time, I did not think about writing a book but rather about going to the media, perhaps an article in a newspaper or something like a news special on TV. After those prayers, I had a strong feeling that after these two meetings, the first on August 22, 2012, with the reconstruction officer from the Collision and Reconstruction Section and the second on August 29, 2012, with the detective and his supervisor from the District Attorney's Office, I should have asked my husband to help me write down reports of these meetings straightaway. I knew we needed to keep good records for our own sake as well as to send to our car insurance company and our lawyer. And maybe it happened because I would need it for this book. I sent the report of these meetings to them on September 4, 2012. We never received a response.

I still wanted to change our lawyer, but my family continued to believe in him. He suggested that we wait for the final report before proceeding. At this time, I also started to learn about computers and concentrate more on improving my English. The process is ongoing, and it has helped me to relearn patience for myself and others, which I had mostly lost after this accident. I know that my family and I have been deeply hurt and that recovery takes time. I understand that it will never be the same anymore without our Lisa. Our relationship with God is tighter than ever and always growing stronger. I believe that God saved Lisa, and He saved us too. We will be together again one day, and I try to keep this on my mind. We now, more than ever, feel that we are constantly under attack by the devil, trapped by the evil of this corrupted worldly system. We are most vulnerable to this evil when we feel the acute hurt of how badly we miss Lisa. I say about these times that I have my "moments" or my "homesick" times, and though it may not convey the depth of what I'm experiencing, it helps anyone understand what I mean. When driving through the streets, I "see" Lisa in almost every car that passes by. When I see mothers out shopping with their daughters, I am reminded of doing the same with Lisa. There are memories in every place we ever went together, and these memories are painful to me now.

At these moments, I feel her hand on my arm, and the presence helps me to calm down. What is very interesting about this is when I have these moments of contact, the hand on my arm doesn't appear right away but instead appears about three minutes later. I think maybe that is how long it takes for the message of me missing her to reach heaven and for her to come and comfort me. She knows my pain. During the investigation, I felt such a hunger for connection with her that I needed it more and more. I prayed and Ben said he would pray for me too, that I would see her not only in my visions in dreams, but also when I was awake. I have to remind myself often "to accept what happened and be happy that she is in heaven," but it is difficult to accept, and even more difficult to be happy, though I know it is the direction that I must turn to. The biggest difficulty for me and my family is the pain of being separated from Lisa, of accepting her temporary departure from life here, as long or short as our separation may be. Any sudden change is difficult to accept, especially when it is tragic. I try to think about our separation from God's presence through sin, how awful it was for the first man, Adam, and his wife, Eve. Because of their disobedience,

God had to go away from their presence. Or for Jesus when He was dying for our sins on the cross and called to his Heavenly Father, "Why have you forsaken me?" Or for Jesus's mother, Mary, to watch her son dying. How painful this must have been. I am not alone with my pain. God knows that separations hurt. It's important for me to understand the situation I am in. I am in pain, but I am not alone. Jesus promised his followers in Matthew 28:20 (NLT), "And be sure of this: I am with you always, even to the end of the age."

The rest of the summer, we spent preparing Ben for a new job in Canada. We continued going to La Salette Shrine in Attleboro in the morning for prayer and meditation, which had a positive effect on us. We needed this separation from the world to listen quietly to the calmness of nature, smell the warm summer flowers, feel the refreshing breeze on our skin, and look up at the blue sky when sitting on a bench under a tree. It was like God was comforting us, even with the weather because it was perfect for that time of year, and not too hot. The longing for our daughter did not leave us for a moment, but prayer definitely alleviated our sorrow for the rest of the day. We continued going to our church, but the quaintness and calmness was the best thing for us then, and we felt closer to God when we prayed together in this special isolated place.

## Back to Normal

O God, you are my God; I earnestly search for you.

—Psalm 63:1 (NLT)

The summer quickly reached its end. On September 17, 2012, Ben had to go to Kitimat, Canada, for his new job. It was very hard for us to leave each other, and we promised not to cry, but we did. It would be a very challenging time for both of us. He was going to a completely new environment where he barely knew anybody. He knew that they wondered if he would be strong enough to handle the stress of his responsibilities at work. Sometimes when he was working, he would suddenly feel the longing for Lisa, and it was not possible for him to hold back tears. He would pretend that he had to use eye drops for his eyes or he'd go to the bathroom, but it was very tough. He told me that usually, when he returned from work to his bedroom at the work camp where he was living now, he would cry into the pillow so that nobody would hear him. He needed to relieve his sorrow somehow, which he was holding all day. The nights were the worst. Often, he didn't sleep well and had bad dreams about this accident, which woke him up at night drenched in sweat. He told me the books that I'd packed for him—the Bible, *Our Daily Bread*, and a few other Christian books—were his only sources of mental nourishment, which kept him strong. He had some friends there who knew our situation and were good support for him too. Ben found a church in Kitimat and was attending it on Sundays. We called each other often just to say I love you.

When I left the airport after dropping him off for his flight, I was so upset that I got lost on the way home from Boston, and it took me almost three hours when usually it is only a forty-minute drive. When I finally got back, our home was suddenly sad, empty, and quiet. I didn't know what to do. To avoid the emptiness of our house, I went grocery shopping and took this very slowly. *Now is the time to organize this mess and get the accident case in order,* I thought. It would keep me busy and give me a feeling of purpose.

I am usually easily discouraged, and it would be something new to learn, but Lisa motivated me. When the business people who took care of my daughter's car accident case saw my irritation about how the investigation was turning out, they would often say, "Why do you bother? She will not come back to you anyway!" But one day, I will go to her, to my beloved daughter who is waiting for me; and when I finally am able to look into her eyes, I want to be able to tell her, "I love you. I did not give up on you. Never, to the end of my life." Because then it will be the beginning of forever.

This first year of mourning was a year of humble repentance and full of miracles. I believe that God encouraged and rewarded us because we chose to honor and respect our Heavenly Holy Father. We trust Him and find hope in Him. Ben is often seeing rainbows.

When he was flying to Canada for his new job, he was depressed and worried that the project he was assigned to work on would be canceled. He was informed that it was uncertain whether or not it would proceed. He was thinking about this when he saw a rainbow on the wing of the airplane. It encouraged him greatly, and he knew that everything would be all right. I told him about the time when Lisa and I were flying to visit him in Australia six months before her accident, when she pointed out a rainbow on the airplane's wing. I'd never seen anything like it. I was excited and told her that I thought *it was a sign from God that everything would be okay.* A rainbow is a symbol of hope, and from then on, Ben saw them often. He always called me or sent me picture messages of them to share these little sweet miracles with me. We believed these rainbows were signs from Lisa.

Two months later, when Ben came back from Canada for Thanksgiving on the escalator at the airport (probably due to the light from a window or something else) a rainbow was the first thing to welcome him back home.

While Ben was in Canada, I struggled with my grieving and was forced to face reality alone. It is hard to go from being with someone whom you love more than your own life all the time to coping with her sudden—in what seemed like the blink of an eye—disappearance. I knew where she is, but separation from her was "killing" me.

Every morning, I'd drag myself to Lisa's room and pray and cry in earnest. Besides meditating and reading the Bible, it was also very crucial for me to read some encouraging Christian books. It helped to know how other people going through similar circumstances were able to cope with their struggles and deal with these issues. It isn't an easy or fast process. The key is patience. It took me a long time before I could focus on the things I had to do each day, but after these morning preparations, I felt stronger every day.

Because prayer and meditation was what I was doing first thing when I woke up at that time, I often took showers very late. Long showers also helped me to relax from grieving.

Water has the amazing power to relieve stress, and I often knelt and prayed while the warm water ran with my heavy tears down the drain, lightening my burden. Still, I begged God to let me see Lisa while I was awake.

In church, my fellow church members did not understand my sensitivity, and I did not understand myself either. I would often overreact too. When someone would ask how I was feeling, I would kindly but firmly shoot the question back at them. "I am fine," I would say. "But how are you feeling?" Or if they asked me about Ben and how he was doing, I would answer, "He is fine." I didn't want to talk to anybody about how we were feeling.

A few times at the beginning of Mass, I had to leave the church when the worship music started. A stream of tears poured from me uncontrollably accompanied by sobs. Except for with my family, I didn't feel comfortable talking about my feelings. I didn't want to attend any grief-support groups because I was very sensitive, and I worried I would go through everyone else's pain as well. I was afraid that it would make me stay focused on negativity and would not help the healing process for me. I was too emotional after the shock of the news that my beloved daughter had been killed in the car accident. I felt that I needed a positive, calm atmosphere and a different subject to talk about, so instead, I joined a painting group. It helped me find balance, and I enjoyed it.

I wanted God to heal me, and I believed that He would. The way He is leading me and guiding me now, through all my circumstances, is encouraging and hopeful. I was thinking that *our faith would always be tested for the rest of our lives on earth*. We should be ready to accept that. Am

I ready? I know also that this kind of question, like the question why, has no answers, so I don't bother to ask.

"Give your burden to the Lord, and he will take care of you. He will not permit the godly to slip and fall" (Psalm 55:22, NLT).

## The Fourth Vision: Awake

O God: "I lie awake thinking of you, meditating
on you through the night."

—Psalm 63:6 (NLT)

The fourth vision of Lisa happened a week after Ben left home for his new job in Canada. I was not only praying, meditating, and reading the Bible in the morning but also in the evening now. I would pray in my daughter's room before bedtime, still begging God for one more vision. I missed her so much that I asked God to take me too. Her hand on my arm helped to calm me, but it wasn't enough. Though I was grateful and thankful for these signs, the pain in my soul was still unbearable.

Somehow, after praying, most of my nights were peaceful. I had dreams, and they were good and even encouraging. One night, however, something woke me up from my sleep. I opened my eyes, and in the darkness, I saw a vertical irregular crack in the air, like a small opening. It looked as if a veil was being pushed away. From this opening, a soft white light was pouring out as if a door was opening slightly to a room beyond with the lights on. From the top of this crack, I saw many emerging bright shapes, like faces that were appearing one over another, no single one clearly defined. I knew that this was the answer to my many prayers.

"Lisa?" I called. Then I saw her face rise from the veil. She looked different than she had in my visions of her, more spirit than form, and she appeared very peaceful, looking at me with deep love as if she were the mother and I, the daughter. It was only a moment before this opening closed, but from it, I heard her voice repeating, "I am sorry. I am sorry. I am sorry." The voice was so clear that it was as if she was near me, but it sounded as if it was coming from far away. It was so alive, so warm, natural, and real.

"She is alive!" I kept thinking. "I heard her!" It was such a weird feeling to know that she had passed away, and yet I saw and even heard her! It was as if two different dimensions and two different lives had met.

Thinking about this vision, it occurred to me that the many faces that appeared may have been companions of Lisa's. I think that Lisa wasn't alone, and perhaps she had spoken about us, so her curious companions were peeking at me until I called her name. She loved people and was very social, so it made perfect sense that she still is. I thank God for showing me that Lisa has many friends in heaven. I believe Lisa was apologizing for leaving me, telling me that she was sorry for what was happening and that I was suffering. This also is bringing to my mind Lisa's first car accident in January 2011, during a heavy snowstorm in January. We were very upset that our daughter decided to drive to her after school job in such bad weather conditions. It was already dark, and the surface on the highway was icy and slippery when Lisa was driving home from her afternoon work. She hit the black ice and slipped off the highway, then after, when spinning around on the snowy pavement, her car bumped into the Jersey barrier, causing damage to itself. Lisa was very blessed that she was okay.

I found out about this accident after I arrived home from grocery shopping. I went to Lisa's room and saw her sitting on her bed deeply sad. When she saw me, she started to apologize: "I am sorry, I am sorry, I am sorry," she repeated three times as I interrupted her.

"It wasn't your fault," I repeated a few times to calm her down. "It was a car accident, and it can happen to anybody. It's very bad weather. I am so happy that you are okay," I said as I was embracing her in my arms.

This fourth vision with Lisa did not give me peace till it hit me. As I've mentioned, I don't believe in coincidence. There had to be a reason she was in this vision again, repeating the same thing three times that she is sorry, just as she had after her first car accident: Lisa was giving me a message, that this second car accident also wasn't her fault. During my morning time with our Heavenly Father the next day, I thanked God for answering my prayers, that I saw her while I was awake and asked Him why Lisa looked different during my first and my recent vision. I felt the reply, "We don't have airplanes in heaven," which I thought was very funny. In my first vision, she lost her body and Jesus took her spirit to his kingdom, so I saw her spirit. In the fourth vision, she came to me in spirit too.

> As they rode along, they came to some water, and the eunuch said, "Look! There's water! Why can't I be baptized?" And they went down into the water, and Philip baptized him. When they came up out of the water the Spirit of the Lord caught Philip away. The eunuch never saw him again.... Meanwhile, Philip found himself farther north at the city of Azotus! He preached the Good News there and in every city along the way until he came to Caesarea. (Acts 8:36–40, NLT)

Wow, talk about travel! Traveling in spirit is a mystery for me, but I believe this is what Lisa did in both my first and last visions of her. In the Bible, it says that our spirit will have a new body in heaven. I believe it will be a powerful body—strong, radiating with energy that emanates like freshness of spring, always young and beautiful—like Lisa's in my second and third visions, which I had when I was sleeping. I imagine Jesus after the resurrection, and I understand why he wasn't easily recognized. He was in his new heavenly body. From disciples' reaction when they saw Him after His resurrection in the Bible, I had reason to believe that they were astounded.

> That same day two of Jesus' followers were walking to the village of Emmaus.... Suddenly, Jesus himself came along and joined them and began walking beside them. But they didn't know who he was. (Luke 24:13, 15, 16; NLT)

> As they sat down to eat, he took a small loaf of bread, asked God's blessing on it, broke it, then gave it to them. Suddenly, their eyes were opened, and they recognized him. And at that moment he disappeared! (Luke 24:30–31, NLT)

> And just as they were telling about it, Jesus himself was suddenly standing there among them. (Luke 24:36, NLT)

> Then Jesus led them to Bethany, and lifting his hands to heaven, he blessed them. While he was blessing them, he left them and was taken up to heaven. (Luke 24:50–51, NLT)

After my daughter's accident, I had the desire to go to the planetarium. I learned there that, according to scientists, we only perceive a small portion of our world. It seems to me that, practically, we are almost blind and deaf. When we cannot see bacteria, some of which can even kill us, how can we think that we can understand heaven? There's still so much to discover here on earth, and there always will be. I've realized that humans cannot create anything that already exists. We are just discoverers, and it depends on our gifts or talents what kind of discovery we could make, then we can choose to use it for good or evil. Life is short, and we have human limitations, which only faith can overcome. We need to trust God and put our hope in Him. After I saw this wonderful universe at the planetarium, it refreshed my realization of just how mighty my Creator is. I am His very tiny creature, and He loves me.

> Now we know only a little, and even the gift of prophecy reveals little…. Now we see things imperfectly as in poor mirror, but then we will see everything with perfect clarity. All that I know now is partial and incomplete, but then I will know everything completely, just as God knows me now. (1 Corinthians 13:9, 12; NLT)

# To Turn the Tables

"The unfailing love of the Lord never ends.
By His mercies we have been kept from complete
destruction.
Great is His faithfulness. His mercies begin afresh
each day."

—Lamentation 3:22–23 (NLT)

## Ben's Relatives

When Ben went to Canada for his new job, I was left alone for the next eight weeks until he came back home for his two-week rotation. I struggled with a lot of fear at this time, and I could see in their eyes and from their behaviors that Ben and Peter did too. I can't even imagine people in a situation like ours without Jesus to support them.

Three years before Lisa's car accident, my husband's aunt and uncle in Germany had their daughter Lola die suddenly in their arms just after dinner one Sunday night. It happened in front of her three young children and her husband, Martin. Ben's uncle did everything he could think of to try and save his daughter's life, including rescue breathing and chest compressions until the ambulance came, but the medics pronounced her dead when they arrived. Lola was forty-two years old. She had a massive heart attack and died in an instant. We were very sorry for them and sad for their loss. I knew their daughter. She was lovely, kind, and sweet like Lisa, but we didn't understand how critical this tragedy was for them at the time. Later, during our own hardship, we learned from other relatives that Ben's aunt was in very poor health. We asked about their faith in God. "They have no faith," we heard. Our other relatives hoped that we could try and help them, so we promised we would. My husband's uncle and aunt are very nice people, and I told Ben that I would talk to his aunt. I thought it would be easier for me to talk to her than it would be for Ben, but it wasn't. I'd never spoken with someone so bitter and angry with God. When I told her how faith in God was helping us, she was angry and did not believe me but stubbornly insisted that my own strong character made me resilient. It hurt me to hear that because I knew it was not true.

I thought, *She is much stronger that I am. I am so weak that I can't trust or rely on myself anymore. I need someone really strong like the Son of God to help me.*

But I wasn't successful, and I was disappointed with myself that I was unable to help.

"Ben," I said to my husband, "I am worried about them. We will pray for them, and you have to talk with your aunt." It took a while, but later, during the time we spent fasting and praying for Lisa's car accident case, God reminded Ben to call. He did, and his uncle picked up the phone. He told Ben that his aunt was very sick in the hospital and that the doctors expected that she'd be there for a month. The doctors detected some spots on her brain. It wasn't cancer; they didn't know what it was. Doctors thought that it could have been from the constant stress she'd been under. She lost half of her body weight and was incredibly dizzy, and Ben's uncle was very worried about her. He was surprised to hear that we were doing relatively okay. Ben talked about our faith in God, but it was very hard at the beginning because of his uncle's bitterness and anger. Slowly, he began to listen. Ben brought some hope into the conversation, and his uncle said he would share this with his wife too. She was visiting many doctors and counselors and taking antidepressants, and nothing helped her. Ben's uncle was amazed that we hadn't sought any outside help, that God was all we relied on. At the end of their conversation, Ben's uncle was happy that they'd talked. Ben promised him he'd call more often. This example from Ben's relatives reminded me how important it is to focus on God's promises. Keep your eyes on Jesus always! This was the lesson I learned from my first vision of Lisa. He is our only hope, and He is better than anybody, anything! This was from my second vision of my daughter.

## Peter's Vision: The Angel

Then there was war in heaven. Michael and the
angels under his command fought the dragon
(devil) and the dragon lost the battle and was
forced out of heaven.

—Rev.12:7–8 (NLT)

It had been more than twelve weeks since Lisa's accident, and Ben and I had been apart for over three weeks. Thank God that Peter was living nearby and we were able to still have breakfast together often. Peter was missing his sister very much. He tried to hide this, but his eyes were always red. It wasn't possible to talk about Lisa without both of us crying. He bought a beautiful crystal statue of an angel than has a place to put Lisa's picture in, with its wings encircling her.

October 2012 was my first birthday without my daughter, and I wanted the day to be very calm. Most of this day, I spent with my son. I tried to keep busy by organizing my home, reading Christian books, and learning to use the computer. I tried avoiding my relatives and friends because I preferred taking time for quiet prayers and meditation so that I might discover what God wanted me to do next. Somehow, I began worrying about Peter, and one morning after my birthday, I woke up very weary. After a while, the stress accumulated too much in me, and I felt that I had to unload it and give it to Jesus in prayer.

In my bed, I prayed for Peter for a long time. I went to Lisa's room and continued, then I meditated on the Bible. It was close to one in the afternoon when I finally took my long shower, and on my knees, I still kept praying for him. I begged God to keep Peter safe. I begged God that I wouldn't have to go through that kind of sorrow anymore in the future; I wanted to die instead. I cried and prayed and let the water run over my shoulders, relaxing me.

About half an hour after I got out of the shower, Peter called me with exhilaration in his voice.

"Mom," he said, "I'm coming over. I have to tell you something. I had a vision. It was an angel."

"What! How did it happen?" I asked.

"I'm coming over," Peter answered impatiently.

As soon as Peter got in the house, I jumped to meet him.

"Tell me, P. When did it happen?" I asked. I noticed his face was lit up, happiness and excitement radiating from him.

"I woke up late today," Peter said. "And I was quickly going through my usual routine, getting ready for my second shift at work. Then I took a shower. Sometimes, I like to relax and sit with my eyes closed and just feel the warm water on me and listen to it running."

I smiled.

"Then suddenly, I felt like somebody was gently massaging my arms and back. I wasn't scared though. It felt so pleasant, and I didn't want it to disappear, so I didn't move."

"You felt a massage?" I asked surprised.

"Yes," Peter continued. "And I began to feel really strong. It was very powerful, this sense that I shouldn't be afraid of anything. I also experienced an incredible feeling of peace and joy at the same time. I've never felt that way before. I didn't think that kind of peace existed here on earth. I heard a gentle voice in my head saying, 'You are safe. You are safe.' When I opened my eyes, I saw huge, solid wings around me. I look up, and coming up to the ceiling was a beautiful face that looked like it was carved from white marble. It was looking up towards heaven, and this angel was cast in a soft white light. The massage lasted for a while and then slowly disappeared."

I hugged my son and cried. My prayers for Peter were answered, and it couldn't have come in a better way.

"What time did you take your shower, P?" I asked.

"About one o'clock," he answered, surprised.

"Me too," I told him. I explained how I prayed for him.

"Mom, I thought that angels were girls, but my angel's face looked more like a man's face," Peter said.

I smiled and told him, "Peter, if you read the Bible, you'll see that it never mentioned any women angels but only men."

He was glad to hear that. I thought about what Peter felt during this experience—*the power of strength and boldness and the power of peace and joy.* In my visions of Lisa, this power of peace and joy, which radiated from her body in a warm, bright, amber light, was beautiful and couldn't be expressed in words. I understand that this is the kind of body the followers of Christ will have in heaven.

"For we will not be spirits without bodies, but we will put on new heavenly bodies" (2 Cor. 5:3, NLT). Peter told me that he missed this feeling and he wished he could feel this all the time. The vision took his fear of death away. He knows where he will go. But we are still here in this dying word, and Jesus wants us to lead lives that are abounding in love, peace, and joy to proclaim to everyone that His kingdom is near. Peter's vision helped to refocus us on the positive aspects of life in Christ, and we began trying to do just that. I even started writing poems and songs again, but they were still full of pain.

"Crying Eyes"

Crying eyes are sad
When they cry from sorrow
They don't look for hope
for a bright tomorrow
They don't want to stop
Until sorrow abates
by bending down the knees
and folding hands in faith.

## Under Attack

> So that at the name of Jesus every knee will bow,
> in heaven and on earth and under the earth, and
> every tongue will confess that Jesus Christ is Lord,
> to the glory of God the Father.
>
> —Philippians 2:10 (NLT)

We knew recovering from this kind of tragedy would take time, and we trusted Jesus Christ and thanked Him for every miracle and vision we'd been given. The wounds in us were deep and only people who go through this kind of sorrow can understand it fully. Over and over, we were hit with more pain from this cruel world.

October flew by. It was easier because of Peter's vision. And the beginning of November was exciting because I was looking forward to Ben returning from Canada for Thanksgiving. The holidays are now different from when Lisa was alive, and it will never be the same. Peter was working that afternoon, and Ben and I went to the movies. Ben's two weeks passed by fast, and he left for work in Canada again.

At the end of November 2012, about one month before Christmas, we got, from our car insurance, a copy of the first report of Lisa's car accident written by a state trooper who was at the car accident scene.

My husband and son were in shock. They had hoped that it would have been done more fairly. I couldn't read this report at first. I needed time to calm down. Ben promised that we would go through this report together when he came back for his next rotation. He wanted to read it over. He didn't have enough time to read through it properly while he was home.

It was just four months after the accident, and everything was still very fresh. We were living under extreme pressure. Ben had been working in Canada for two months already and was struggling to supervise our issues with this case from a distance while also juggling his new work. During the height of this emotional disaster, we got very good news from Ben's company; they would be giving Ben extra time off for Christmas. I was surprised by their compassion and was very grateful. It is rare to see this sort of compassion in business. We thanked God and prayed for my husband's company. Peter often visited me for a short time. He wasn't easy to talk with, but every day, we shared our thoughts about Bible scriptures and about the booklet *Our Daily Bread* via e-mail or on the phone. This lifted my spirit up for rest of the day. As excited as I was that Ben would come home for Christmas, I did not want to decorate our home because it was so sad that Lisa couldn't celebrate this holiday with us. I didn't go a single day without crying; missing Lisa was very painful.

Days grew shorter, and the darkness was gloomy. In New England, this time of year is monotonous. It did not seem a suitable atmosphere for this beautiful holiday for me now.

Everyone mentioned how hard it would be for my family to be without our Lisa this first Christmas, but this only brought to my attention that this holiday isn't about our daughter or about us; it is about Jesus, and it shouldn't be hard. So I was the first person in my neighborhood to decorate my house, and I was ready to celebrate. But the devil did not like this, and a week before Christmas, our car insurance informed us that they also received a forensic medical report concerning Lisa. We requested they send us a copy. Since the police and our lawyer did not answer any of our letters or e-mails, we wanted to have a peaceful break during this important holiday. We thought it was odd that we got both the police report and the forensic medical report, which should have come from Washington DC or the state police directly, from our car insurance alone. Our car insurance was very surprised that we hadn't gotten anything from the state police. The forensic medical report was a disaster and a shock for us. It contradicted itself, was very confusing, and made no sense.

"Ben," I said when he arrived home the day before New Year's Eve 2013, "we will not spoil Christmas. We will celebrate and take care of this after the holiday." I reminded my family and myself that it was Jesus's birthday, and I decided to be happy, for Him. It was a nice Christmas. As it had been before, Lisa's hand was on my shoulder for the entire day—while I cooked, ate, opened presents, enjoyed time with my family, and, at the end, when we prayed. I felt peaceful and content.

## Twenty-One Days of Fasting and My Report for Police

> Then no one will suspect you are fasting, except your Father, who knows what you do in secret. And your Father, who knows all secrets, will reward you.
>
> —Matthew 7:18 (NLT)

Because of the generous extra time off he was given near the holidays, Ben was not away long. He was set to come home from his rotation on January 26, 2013. In the meantime, I didn't know what to do with this devastating report. At this time, I heard on the TBN program *Kingdom Connection* about twenty-one days of fasting. I had fasted before, but not for as long. After listening to people's testimonies, I figured that it could not hurt to try because I didn't know how to do anything else. I called Ben and asked him if he would do it with me. For him, it would only be the first three days after he arrived back home. I bought J. Franklin's book called *Fasting* and started my first, long, twenty-one-day fast on January 14 for my daughter's car accident case. I prayed and begged God to close this awful case. I was constantly worried about who might take advantage of our situation. We could lose everything. After all, Lisa's car was in my name, and we knew that we were the only ones in this car accident claim to have good car insurance and a home. When our lawyer first met us, he was only interested in our insurance policy. It seemed to me that he wasn't paying too much attention to the car accident and that we wanted to defend our daughter.

I prayed for truth, and again, God reminded me to go to the public. But how? What should I do? I got the idea of making a website. I'd just learned how to use the computer, and the thought of making a website was terrifying to me. I had to find somebody who would help me. I prayed for God's justice and waited. Something about the first report did not give me peace. We learned that the first report by the State Trooper who was at the accident scene was not final. The final piece would be a report by the reconstruction officer with whom we talked previously and who would close the case, and we wanted to talk with him again. I had a hope that something would change for the better, because he is a Christian. I procrastinated reading this first report, but I knew that we should respond to it quickly. I asked

Ben to do it for me so that I could just read his statement and sign. He understood my frustration and promised to help me, but only after I read the police report.

"You have to read it, Dana," Ben said to me. "You know the truth. Remember God loves you, and He already showed you that He is on your side." Finally, I got up the courage and read this first report. At the beginning of this report, they mentioned briefly that they had some criminal activity on Route 24 South, in Raynham, at the time the car accident happened. Immediately, I recalled my first conversation with the state police trooper who came to my door that morning. He told me that they'd been chasing a bad guy and lost him in the Brockton area around Exit 18. They suspected he was responsible for this crash, running the wrong direction on the highway to Exit 15, to Raynham. They also mentioned in this report three different witnesses who saw some car running in the wrong direction on the highway. We were like prey, deceived by fear and pain, misled by "business" people. I called the state police reconstruction section office, but the reconstruction officer wasn't there, so I left a message for him straight and clear. Ben tried to contact them too, but nobody answered his calls and e-mails. During my eighth day of fasting, I sent a report to the reconstruction section via e-mail.

To Lieutenant and Reconstruction Officer

I have just received the first police report from the trooper who was on the accident scene, which was written over 3 months after the accident on 10/17/12.

I tried to call you both, but never received any calls back, which is why I am writing this e-mail.

This report contains statements from all of the people involved in this accident. After reading their statements in detail, I see that no one reported witnessing Lisa B., my daughter, driving in the wrong direction or causing this accident. Even the wife of the driver of the pickup truck (who was killed in this accident) claims that she was awake at the time of the crash and was listening to music when it happened, but did not see any headlights coming from the opposite direction at them. She did not know if they were driving in the middle or the left lane, or what caused the crash, but she felt their car hit something like a wall and start to spin, coming to a stop facing the jersey barrier.

I am very surprised that even though every witness from this accident mentioned a tractor trailer being involved, the police report makes no mention of it. Additionally, the police sketch shows in great detail how all the cars were positioned during this accident, but does not include the tractor trailer. I do not understand how the information was gathered for this sketch since the witnesses state something completely different, as do the photos from the accident.

You made another statement that somebody made a U-Turn just before exit 17 and started to drive in the opposite direction, and you believe it was Lisa's car.

In this police report, three of the witnesses state that they saw a car already driving in the opposite direction from exit 18 in the Brockton area. It is very possible that this car started the whole crash and escaped unnoticed while the other cars, trying to avoid him, started to brake and spin and got into this terrible crash.

Officers, I am the desperate mother of the girl who was killed in this crash, and I know that nothing will bring her back to us, but I am looking for what really happened that night, and I will never give up. However, the deeper I go into this investigation, the more I see that we cannot find any clear, true evidence, and we have no witnesses who can clearly explain how this whole crash happened. There were cars involved in this crash that ran away from the accident scene; there was a driver who didn't even have a valid driver's license, and had a police warrant out for his arrest in Fall River. He was arrested right after the accident. Then there were the witness statements: one person supposedly saw someone make a U-turn just before exit 17 and start driving back against oncoming traffic, while many other witnesses reported having seen a car driving in the opposite direction north of the accident as early as exit 18 in Brockton. The state trooper who first came to my door mentioned that there'd been a police chase that night at that same time on route 24.

We cannot determine what the sequence of all of these crash events was, or how really this whole crash really started based on this information. We do not even know how many cars were truly involved, as there are reports of a few vehicles fleeing the scene. Before you draw any conclusions in the reconstruction report of this accident, every detail I mentioned above must be investigated fully, and your detectives must be 100 % sure, and have indisputable, hard evidence before determining who was really at fault. I would appreciate if you would find time to meet with me again as you promised during our first meeting.

## The End of Fasting

*Your unfailing love is better to me than life itself;*
*how I praise you!*

—Psalm 63:3 (NLT)

We heard no response to any of our calls, e-mails, or my letter. They were completely mute to us. I didn't know if that was even right.

Shouldn't they have an obligation to keep crash victims' families informed? Aren't there laws and rules about this? Don't we have any rights as Lisa's parents and next of kin to receive any answer to these questions? Why are we being treated like that? I did not understand.

Ben was fasting for three days with me, as he promised, and we prayed together in the morning and evening in our daughter's room. On the morning of my last day of fasting, as I was praying with Ben, I asked God again to close Lisa's accident case. My husband got frustrated and interrupted me.

"Dana," he said, "it takes time, sometimes even a few years to close such a complex car accident case!"

I wasn't very happy about his interruption or his pessimism.

"No, Ben!" I yelled. "God can close this case right now if he wants! I am sure this case is closed already! Call the insurance company. You will see!"

I don't know why I was so sure, but passion for God and the belief that He was answering my prayers was burning in me.

"Go call," I hustled him. "Go!"

"Okay," Ben said reluctantly. He walked to the next room to call our insurance while I remained in Lisa's room to finish my prayers. I will never forget his face when he walked back in a moment later.

"The case is closed," he said. We were so surprised that we weren't sure if we should be happy or not. Certainly, it felt as if there was a burden of pressure taken off us at least.

We praised and thanked God for closing the case, and we were curious how it happened.

When my end of fasting came closer, I realized that I'd made a mistake in planning my fasting period. The end of it was on my son's birthday, at the beginning of February 2013. We went to a very nice restaurant, and everyone was eating, except for me. The food smelled and looked delicious, but it was my twenty-first day, and I couldn't ruin it, especially not after God had answered my prayers. The case was closed! We were all so relieved.

## How It Was Closed

Ears to hear and eyes to see—both are gifts from the Lord.

—Prov.21:12 (NLT)

When Ben called our car insurance company and asked about our daughter's car accident case, he was surprised when the voice on the other end sounded amused.

"Congratulations, Mr. Banat, your case is closed! I can't explain anything to you unfortunately. The person who took care of your claim is not working today. She took few days off. Please call later. Maybe next week. Aren't you happy?

We took great care in closing it, Mr. Banat. Please call back in a few days, and she will explain everything."

"Can you send me a copy of the closure?" my husband asked.

"I can't. That claim is not my responsibility, but I want to assure you that you will be pleased with how we handled your claim, Mr. Banat, and I will relay to her that you called and asked for copy of the closure, Mr. Banat," the amused voice said.

We were puzzled. How had it been closed? When? Why had nobody informed us about closing the case? Was that right? We'd come to be very suspicious and distrustful since the newspapers had announced incompatible information in the immediate aftermath of this tragedy.

We called back later as the amused voice had instructed us, but we always got the same strange response: "she" was at a meeting, "she" had just left work early, "she" was at lunch, "she" is too busy and would call us back, but she didn't.

We decided to drive to the car insurance company and talk with her directly, but "she" wasn't available, because "she" had just left again. Finally fed up, we said that we would not go anywhere and wanted to talk to the manager. Our car insurance excused themselves, saying that they had called our lawyer many times but had to leave him a message when he did not answer.

"Why didn't you call us?" I asked.

"We did, but nobody answered," they said.

"I did not get any messages, e-mails, or letters from you," I told them.

The manager said, "Our policy paid a settlement to the woman who lost her husband in this car accident."

We understood, but we were confused as we still did not know the truth. We tried to contact our lawyer to ask him if he knew what was going on, but we didn't receive any answers. We sent a "Thank you" letter to him and prayed to God for truth and justice. The case was closed. One thing was finally over, and I was glad, but the mess still remained.

In the orphanage where I grew up, I learned to be disciplined and organized. For me, this case has been very unclear and jumbled from the start. I knew it would keep me busy to organize the evidence and investigate and help me to still feel useful to my daughter. I also hoped that somehow maybe it would help me to adjust slowly to live with her absence. At first, it wasn't clear to us why we didn't get the final report from the officer at the State Police Collision Analysis & Reconstruction Section before the case was closed. At the beginning of this case, we were informed about every detail of the case from our lawyer and our car insurance company, as it should be. When I learned that our car insurance had closed this case between them and the district attorney's office, I asked our car insurance if they'd received the final report from the reconstruction officer, and they said no. They had only gotten the first report, and our car insurance sent a copy of this first report to us too. Afterwards, an associate from the reconstruction office answered my e-mail. "Also the case is closed, but that doesn't mean we will not do our final report." I was confused. If something is closed, shouldn't it be *completely* closed? Why was it closed before the final report was even issued? I wondered, *Is this right?*

## Website and Vision

We can gather our thought, but the Lord gives the
right answer.

—Proverbs 16:1 (NLT)

We weren't sure what else to expect. I felt as if they were
taking advantage of our situation and distress from this
tragedy and keeping us in fear. I trusted God and decided
to not be afraid to stand up for the truth.

> Stand your ground, putting on the sturdy belt of
> truth and the body armor of God's righteousness.
> For shoes, put on the peace that comes from Good
> News, so that you will be fully prepared. In every
> battle you will need faith as your shield to stop
> the fiery arrows aimed at you by satan. (Ephesians
> 6:14–16, NLT)

Ben was sorry that he wasn't helpful and supportive
enough in this case. He was too far from it and too busy
with his new work in Canada. The two-week break that
Ben had from work every two months was not enough
time to do everything that we planned to do: repairing our
house, doctors' appointments, bills, taxes, some important
meetings. The to-do list was never ending. One Sunday,
during worship in church, the pastor asked attendees to
bring up anything we were struggling with so that everyone
could pray to God with our struggles in mind. I asked our
congregation if somebody would be willing to help me
create a website for our case. Everybody in my church knew
what I was going through with Lisa's car accident case. For
the sake of truth, I talked about this often—with neighbors,

in churches, to everyone I knew, even to strangers in stores. The worst thing I could have done would have been to be silent and closed up at home. I knew that from God.

A young man came to me after the service and told me that he could do it. We scheduled a meeting. The night before he was scheduled to come over, I had a vision. I didn't see anything. It was dark, but I knew I was in some huge place like a cathedral because I felt it and heard it echoing. It seemed to me like a vast group of people were gathered there, talking, laughing like a crowd at a Christmas party. I paid more attention, trying to listen closer, hoping that maybe I would hear my daughter. The more attention I paid to listening, the more clearly I began to hear her. She was having a good time! She was talking and laughing! I was very alert, thinking, *Do I really hear her?*

"You hear me," Lisa's amused voice answered. "You hear me," she repeated. "You hear me. Do bigos."

This vision happened just before I woke up. It didn't even feel like I was sleeping. What did she mean by "make bigos"? Bigos is very popular in Europe, a tasty sauerkraut-and-meat dish, which happens to be my husband's favorite. Ben had just come back home from his rotation, so I thought, *If God is telling me through my daughter to make bigos, I better make bigos!* I marched to my kitchen early in the morning and began to cook.

"Wow! What smells so good?" my husband asked happily as he walked downstairs from our bedroom.

"Bigos," I answered.

He looked very surprised. He told me that he'd had a craving for bigos and was dreaming about it for a very long time. He was even happier to discover the reason why I was cooking it. The whole house was filled with the tasty aroma of bigos when the young man arrived to help with my website.

"What is it?" he asked.

"Do you want to try?" I asked.

"No, I really don't like a cabbage."

"You will like this one! Just try it," I urged him. Not only did he like it, but he asked me if he could take it home. I was happy to give it to him. I shared my story with him about the vision I'd had about the bigos.

I hoped that this website would help me to protect the truth of my daughter's innocence, and that maybe it would help me find some witnesses. I ordered T-shirts with my website's caption on them. For a few months, I made thousands of copies of fliers. I gave them out in churches and malls. I even put them on cars, which was sometimes humiliating. I was chased and cursed at, but also hugged by strangers, who cried and prayed with me; some shared their own tragic stories with me. It was a very interesting experience, and I always looked forward to meeting new people and talking to them. It gave me the opportunity to share my visions and talk about God. People were amazed with what I was doing and listened to me. I recognized that many people had their own troubles, and they easily opened up to me. They were looking for compassion and understanding from somebody who was hurting too.

My sister, Jola, tried to help me by distributing the fliers with me in the area where she lived. Then we shared our experiences. She tried to support me in any way she could think of—from visiting me and calling me often to talking with people who could help me with my case, "spoiling" me with presents and lavishing warm words. This kind of publication eventually became expensive and exhausting.

Between distributing fliers, I was also meeting with lawyers. I knew that I couldn't go on like that for too long. A newspaper reporter called, and she offered to help me.

"What do you want to do?" I asked.

"Go to the police for an answer," she said.

I told her I didn't think it was a good idea at that time. I didn't want a war or a ping-pong game. "I don't want my family to hurt more," I told her. "And besides, they're still withholding their final reconstruction report, so I will wait."

## Next Stroke

> The human spirit can endure a sick body, but who
> can bear it if the spirit is crushed?
>
> —Proverbs 18:14 (NLT)

I wondered if I should include this "thing" that happened to me while I was writing the fifth chapter of this book. This was when I was writing about our uncle and aunt from Germany and their poor health condition. But when it happened, it was probably on purpose. Many years ago, we invited a young Polish priest who had just been assigned to our parish to our house. Somehow, the conversation turned to crying. He said that grieving people make very "weird" wry faces when they cry, which aren't possible to even imitate.

Now I would say to him, "Surely, you have to be deeply hurt to make such a face! You can't imitate a soul in pain!"

When grieving people cry, especially those who have lost their children, they cry with their entire body. When it continues for a long enough time, it can really hurt. Pressure pushes up against the abdomen and strains the stomach.

That's why I got the message from God to "accept what happened and be happy that she is in heaven." Despite that, I was still crying every day until I got hurt. My body couldn't take this pressure anymore, and I got a hernia. Now, I knew I needed to learn to control my stress—the pain of missing my daughter—and learn to be happy that she is in heaven!

# Struggling in the Worldly System

Then Jesus told him, "I have come to judge the world. I have come to give sight to the blind and to show those who think they see that they are blind."

—John 9:39 (NLT)

## A Stirring in the Devil's Nest

I met with thirteen different lawyers altogether, and they all basically suggested the same course of action. Usually their interest in the case decreased substantially when they found out that the case was closed and that I was looking to prove that the forensic toxicology report, which I'd gotten from our car insurance and later from the reconstruction officer, was a fraud. They all wanted to start the entire investigation over from scratch, which would have cost a fortune. They also warned me that the investigation would take a very long time, would cost a lot, and would not guarantee success. It was very discouraging.

I searched for Christian lawyers on the internet, hoping they may have a more positive view of the case. I did not find any. Most of the lawyers did not have much experience with the subject. None of them wanted to challenge anybody who works for the state police or bother with anybody who works for the state police lab. They tried to discourage me saying that they often have a lot of predictable excuses and very good lawyers too! They kept reiterating that it would be very expensive, complicated, and difficult to prove that this report was fraudulent. They told me that they would need to take this medical report to a forensic expert for evaluation and that some lab investigation might also be necessary. Just for them to agree to start the investigation, they requested around five thousand dollars upfront.

After a few months of those meetings with lawyers, I felt as if I was chasing my tail. I remembered how, when the accident first happened, we prayed to God for help and asked Him to be our lawyer. *Maybe this is why searching for a lawyer is not working*, I thought. I asked God to please guide me and lead me. What should I do?

I started to seek out doctors to speak with this time. *Maybe I don't have to hire a lawyer*, I thought. *I will hire a forensic expert instead!*

I called the lab where my daughter's body samples were supposedly analyzed. To my shock, they had no records of her or anything on file. They had never heard of my daughter, they told me. They claimed that they never had any samples from her or any papers in their files. I called again and talked with Dr. Marta, the director of the lab. She repeated the same things I'd just heard—no memory or record of my daughter's samples. When I called her again to ask her to clarify the forensic toxicology report since her name and signature were on it, she got angry and told me not to call her anymore, that she'd only speak with my lawyer.

I did not know how to proceed. I tried again to find Christian doctors on Google, but it seemed as if all of them had gone off to be missionaries. Having to start somewhere, I contacted my family's primary care doctor, who knew my daughter her whole life, and asked him for help. He wrote a letter sharing his nice opinions about my beloved daughter Lisa, but told me that he couldn't help me. Then I decided to a send letter to a detective at the District Attorney's office about the doubtful authenticity of this forensic medical report. No reply.

I started looking for forensic experts on the internet. There weren't too many in Boston, but I tried to contact some of them. I sensed unwillingness from them. They told me that they usually worked with lawyers.

"Well, I don't have a lawyer. I am a mother," I pleaded to the one nice retired forensic expert as I called him for the third time. Only after I asked him if he was a Christian too, and he answered me yes, did he "secretly" decided to help me. I sent him the two-paged forensic toxicology report on my daughter Lisa, which, at this time, I had from our car insurance. He soon called me back, indignant.

"What did you send me? This isn't a report!" he said. "You have to send me the rest of the report, and I need the autopsy report too! You should also have a blood test..."

"Sir, this is all I got," I told him.

"That is not possible," he said firmly.

"Sir, why I would lie to you?" I asked.

"You are the next of kin. They legally have to send you the real toxicology report, the autopsy report, the blood test, and anything else they have." He instructed me where to ask for them and told me to contact him again once I had them.

I sent a letter to the doctor who had ordered my daughter's toxicology report, Dr. Eve at the chief examiner's office and asked her to send me Lisa's medical blood tests and her autopsy report. After a few weeks, I received exactly the same forensic toxicology report with the attached statement: "Toxicology report only–no autopsy done." It was signed by an associate named Powers, and I wondered about her name. After all these experiences, I looked at those papers very suspiciously, making my husband smile.

I contacted this nice forensic expert again with what I'd received. In this situation, he was very disappointed and felt sorry for me. He said that he could not help me. He told me he was "in" and asked if I understood. I wasn't sure. How could I understand? Did he mean that he belonged to the same association or group? Regardless, I thanked him and talked about God, and I wondered if I could help him be "in." I was disappointed too. It seemed to me that I was trapped in the worldly system and it didn't matter which side I turned to; I couldn't see anyone leading. So I prayed, and slowly, step by step, some ideas came.

I decided to learn about autopsies. It's simple. An autopsy is sometimes called a postmortem checkup. It is a medical examination of a person's body after death. It wasn't difficult to understand why those doctors wanted an autopsy report. Without performing an autopsy—samples taken from body tissue—there is no basis for a forensic toxicology report. It would be like a doctor sending a medical report with a diagnosis of cancer to a patient who never had a medical exam. How could that be decided if no tests were performed?

A forensic toxicology report that is not based on an autopsy can only be fraudulent. I understood that I needed a forensic expert to confirm this obvious fact if I want to legally take off this deceiving report from my daughter Lisa's record.

So I contacted forensic experts from out of state. I reached some from Providence and California and got the same answers. They told me that this report could not be qualified as a toxicology report, and it contained very confusing and contradictory information. Nobody wanted to evaluate it without an autopsy report and wrote statements about it. After praying for guidance, I got another idea. I sent messages and letters to worldwide professional forensic experts in America and Canada with only one question: would an autopsy need to be done for a forensic toxicology report to be filed if the forensic toxicology report stated that the body tissues taken for the test were vitreous humor, eye, and liver?

Eight professional forensic experts answered me.

1. A doctor from the department of pathology at Cambridge Hospital wrote me a letter. "For liver to be taken for toxicology, an autopsy would have to be done."

2. The Pathology F. Consulting Inc. Forensic Pathology, Vancouver, said, "Most often the toxicology is done after the autopsy, which must have been so in this case as the liver was used."

3. Division director, Office of the Chief Medical Examiner said, "To get liver tissue for testing, an autopsy would need to be performed."

4. A forensic pathology consultant said, "Yes. An autopsy needed to be done to at least some degree. First, to access the liver."

5. A forensic pathologist said, "Obtaining vitreous humor would imply that an autopsy was done. It would be terribly damaging to the eye in a living person."

6. A board-certified anatomic and forensic pathologist said, "The answer is yes for a liver sample."

7. California Lab, autopsy/toxicology said, "Submission of vitreous humor and organ specimens implies that an autopsy was done."

8. A pathology expert said, "You cannot get vitreous humor, liver or other tissue without doing an autopsy. The autopsy finding can then be correlated to the toxicology findings. Good luck."

The conclusion that can be drawn from all of these statements is that a toxicology test could not be done without samples taken from a body, and samples couldn't be taken without conducting an autopsy. Since no autopsy was done, the forensic toxicology report was completely without basis!

## The Trap

## Forensic Toxicology Medical Report

Do for others what you would like them to do for you. This is a summary of all that is taught in the law and the prophets.

—Matthew 7:12 (NLT)

I tried to contact lawyers again, but they only wanted to proceed by contacting a forensic expert, which I'd already done. How much information can you possibly get about a report when it states that an autopsy wasn't done? So

I was informed that the lab could have made a mistake. One lawyer told me that he had a similar case with a forensic toxicology report that had the same statement ("presumptive positive") in it, and in that case, the lab had made a mistake. Another lawyer told me that he had a full cabinet of cases related to misleading toxicology reports. I thought, *maybe this is one of the top problems of the twenty-first century—misleading reports.* I went to the computer to look into this issue, and it was shocking for me to find out that many innocent people may be sitting in jail because of these mistakes. It is heartbreaking. In disbelief, I shook my head while I read a bunch of articles. But still I wondered how my daughter's toxicology report could have been mistaken for somebody else's when her samples were never taken and the lab that was supposed to do it and issued this report never had her information on file or heard of her? What a mess!

Again, I was stuck. What next? I felt more alone with this case than ever before, like a shipwreck victim rafting on the ocean. I don't like watching the news on TV, and I don't like politics. I wasn't sure if I should find an investigative reporter for my case or if my family and I were ready for this. What could it accomplish? Was this the kind of publishing that God was pushing me toward? It frightened me, but with my heart still bleeding after my Lisa's departure, and knowing that I wasn't doing anything wrong, I was able to overcome this dread. I was also motivated by my confidence in her innocence. I believe she was a victim in this tragic accident, but because she died without any witnesses, she was taken advantage of and was blamed without basis. I could not be at peace while Lisa remained wrongfully accused; I had to do it. I had to try. I sent a bunch of e-mails and letters to newspapers, TV news, and to investigative reporters, but without any success. I prayed and felt compelled to take a closer look at this medical report. I noticed that it had two addresses on it. One, the ordering location, was Chief examiner's office with the name of the doctor who had ordered this report, Dr. Eve. It was the same office from which I'd received the forensic toxicology report with the statement "No autopsy done." The other address in the header of this report was University Medical Center, Inc. in Booster and the name of the lab director was Dr. Marta, and her associate, Dr. Jonah. The lab director, Dr. Marta, was the person I had called three times before asking about my daughter's information and getting the same answers—they didn't have any. This lab address seemed to be compelling to some of the lawyers and doctors with whom I spoke.

"This test was done at the university lab!" they said. "Not in the state police lab!"

At the time, there were a lot of issues in some of the state police labs in Massachusetts. The University Medical Center lab in Booster had the same troubles with the few independent labs, according to some newspaper reports at the time.

When Ben came home from his rotation at the beginning of November 2013, I asked him to go with me to check out this university lab and talk directly with the lab director, Dr. Marta. It was a forty-minute drive from our home to the lab in Booster. I'd never been there before. The university was huge and looked very nice. It was easy to find the building where the labs were, but when we got there, we were informed that the lab we were looking for was on the third floor and didn't belong to the university.

"The rest of them do, except that one. It's an independent lab."

"So who owns this lab?" I asked, surprised.

"It's a state police lab, ma'am."

"You're kidding me!" I burst.

"No, ma'am. Are you okay?" he asked.

"Thank you. I am okay," I said. But my heart was beating so hard I felt as if it would jump out of my chest.

"We can come in another day, Dana," Ben said when he saw how nervous I was.

"No, we are here already, and I don't want to come back again," I answered.

This lab did not have a sign on its door like the others. A young woman opened the door, but she did not let us in.

"We want to talk with the director of this lab, Dr. Marta," Ben said.

"She is not working here anymore," the young woman answered.

"Where does she work now?" I asked.

"I can't tell you," the young woman answered.

"Can we talk with the manager of this lab?" I asked.

He immediately appeared.

"Yes," he said. On his shirt, I noticed a label with the name that had been listed on my daughter's toxicology report as the associate director, Dr. Jonah. We asked again to speak with the director of the lab, Dr. Marta.

"She is not working here," he said.

"Where can we find her?" we asked. He answered that he didn't know and added, "I am the director of this lab now."

We shortly explained our concerns to him about our daughter's lab report and asked him for an explanation.

"I don't know anything about it, and Dr. Marta isn't working here anymore. You'll have to go to the chief examiner's office," he said.

"They already sent us a letter," I replied. "You don't have any records in your files of what you are doing here?" I asked in disbelief.

"All of Dr. Marta's files went with her," he said in an amused voice.

I felt disappointed and angry. "All her files and documents left with her and cannot be found or retrieved? Is that legal?"

Ben hugged me. "Don't cry, Dana," he said softly. For a moment, we embraced each other, each with the same sorrow in our hearts. We understood each other's pain. I knew that all this was stressful for him too.

We had this conversation with the lab director, Dr. Jonah, in the corridor outside the lab. It turned out that some other people had overheard us because one of them came running after us to inform us that the previous director, Dr. Marta, was now working for the university lab just one floor below. We went to the university's information desk and found out where she worked as well as her phone number.

When we called her, she didn't want to meet with us. She said it wasn't legal. But she agreed to answer our questions over the phone. I was very irritated, but Ben spoke with her in this kind and pleading voice. He told her that in the report, there were statements like "presumptive positive," and he asked her what that means.

"It means that this test is not complete and not final," she said.

"But this report states that it is the final report," Ben said. She encouraged Ben to talk with Dr. Hash from the chief examiner's office lab. Then I wanted to talk with her. She remembered that I had spoken to her in the past, but she did not remember and knew nothing about the forensic report and the case. She asked me if we had the autopsy report, and I said no.

"That's not possible," she said. "What does the death certificate say? It will explain everything if an autopsy was done." She also recommended that I speak with Dr. Hash. We did not have our daughter's death certificate with us so we could not verify this, but when we came back home, we checked it. It clearly stated, "No autopsy done." It was signed by the same Dr. Eve who'd ordered, and whose name was on, my daughter's forensic toxicology report. What a mess! In prayer, I got a warning to not speak with Dr. Hash.

## The Final Report

Anyone who listens to my teaching and obeys me
is wise, like a person who builds
a house on solid rock.

—Matthew 7:24 (NLT)

Nine months after we received the first report and eight months after the case had been completely closed, we got the final report. I was thinking, *Why even bother? It doesn't make any sense to me. It's too late. The case was closed a long time ago and it wouldn't make anything different now.*

When we received this seventy-page report, we noticed it was mostly just a confusing and disorganized collection of information about the condition of the cars involved. It also seemed to contradict information that had been in the first state police report. We noted some adjustments that had been made, which seemed very questionable to us.

The final report was close based on the forensic medical report, and its conclusion was under the caption: OPINION. That "it is the officer's opinion that" my daughter's being "under the influence of alcohol and drugs may have contributed to this collision." (Drugs did not even show in this very questionable forensic medical report!)

With this final report was also Lisa's toxicology report from Booster, the same one which had already been sent to us twice before. The final police report now had an additional footnote stating that Dr. Eve performed a toxicology analysis on my daughter on July 17, 2012, at the chief examiner's office lab, and tissue specimens from Lisa's liver and vitreous humor had been collected and analyzed. (That is to say she did autopsy.) On July 17, 2012, the same Dr. Eve wrote the death certificate, which clearly states that an autopsy was not done. Later on, from the same office, from Dr. Eve, I got a confirmation statement that an autopsy was not done. It is interesting to note that the forensic toxicology report was ordered by Dr. Eve and registered on the same date, July 17, 2012, independent state police lab at the University in Booster, which informed me several times that they never had any samples or any files with Lisa's name on it.

Again I tried to speak with private investigators, but they just advised me to refresh my relationship with lawyers I'd spoken to who would be better equipped to deal with this sort of case. The criminal lawyers referred me to civil rights attorneys who told me that they didn't do these kinds of cases anymore. Not one lawyer was willing to take my case. Instead, I heard all different excuses, even one saying it was the administration that had made a mistake. I asked one of the nice private investigators to look through Lisa's car accident papers. He had a lot of experience with these types of cases, had connections to the media, and was often on *Fox News*. For many years, he was a very popular police officer.

"What do you want? The case is closed," he said.

"I don't think that the investigation of this case was done or closed rightly. It has placed the blame on my daughter Lisa without any substantial evidence, or even one reliable witness. This forensic toxicology report is obviously fraudulent. It states a BAC so high that a nineteen-year-old girl who weighed less than 120 pounds wouldn't even be able to walk, never mind drive, besides, the state trooper, who first came to my house on July 15, said that alcohol was not involved."

The investigator began to carefully read the medical report. Suddenly, he stood straight up out of his chair and said excitedly, "They really *heavily* exaggerated." When he saw this report, he seemed to change his mind. "I can help you," he said. "I can bring *Fox News* here if you can say on camera that they made a mistake." He repeated this a few times. I was surprised and felt resentment.

"I can't do that. I am not sure if this was a mistake. When you bring them, I will tell them the truth, everything I know," I said. For a moment, we looked into each other's eyes, then he changed the subject.

He wanted to start the whole investigation of the case over. He wanted to interrogate my daughter's friends with lie detector tests, but not follow up at all on this false medical report.

"I can't help you with this matter," he said. I did not understand why.

"This matter belongs to this case," I told him.

He told me that I have considerable information, and he asked me what I wanted to do with it.

"I don't know," I answered, but this question triggered me to think. It looks like I should do something. With an article, I wouldn't have enough space to write everything, and God wanted me to go to the public. I tried to refuse thinking about a book; that's ridiculous, I am not qualified for this. *But anybody has the qualification to stand up for truth and honesty.*

I also told him about my faith and the visions I'd had, and he pulled a cross out from his shirt to show me that he was a Christian too. I prayed for him and was happy to share. I tried very hard to find somebody, a "Sherlock Holmes" type, who had a passion to find the truth. I wanted everything to be done right, but I did not sense that the people we'd met were interested in taking any risks to put in the right effort to help me with my daughter's car accident case. I was disappointed with this case, with this "justice," and with the whole world. I felt so gloomy and heavy, as if I was being dragged along with a crowd behind Jesus before his crucifixion. I was tired and didn't want to have any more meetings. When we did, I decided it would be the last one. I'd learned so much in all those meetings, but I'd had enough.

Our last meeting was with Philip, a young engineer with experience in accident reconstructions. He said that it would be impossible to reconstruct this accident so far after the event, but he listened patiently while we described all the trouble we'd had with this case. After Philip looked through all of the papers and reports that I'd given him, he told us that the scenario described in the last report was a possibility; however, many other scenarios were also possible, though they were never taken into consideration. He was very compassionate and sorry that he couldn't help, and I felt it was genuine.

After these meetings, my husband and I needed a break, and we planned to drive to Cape Cod the next day to relax. The night before this trip, Ben woke up from a nightmare and was terrified. When Peter came over for breakfast the next morning, Ben told him about it.

"Last night, I had a nightmare that the police were chasing me and they stopped me three times," he said. We found it funny, but I also took it as a warning to be careful. "Maybe I am thinking about this accident too much," Ben said. As we began our drive home from the Cape, Ben made a mistake and had to turn around. He drove to the side of the road to turn the car when suddenly, from out of nowhere, a police car stopped in front of us.

"You can't turn here!" the officer said, but he let us go with a warning.

"Ben," I said nervously, "your dream is coming true. Please be careful. According to your dream, we should meet them two more times," I said. During our drive home, we spotted them following us on the highway. They drove parallel to us for a moment before taking off ahead. "One more time," I said excitedly. Finally, while we crossed the border out of Cape Cod, we saw them waiting under an overpass. This was the third time.

"Now," I said to Ben, "your nightmare is finished." We both laughed. "Thank you, God, for warning us!"

When we discussed this adventure later, Ben recalled an earlier dream he'd had about Lisa's accident. He dreamed about how it happened, and the dream made sense based on the evidence. He shared this theory during our meeting with the lead detective and his supervisor from the District Attorney's Office on August 29, 2012.

An important fact about the crash is that only Lisa's chest was crushed, but her bottom half and her legs were in good condition. I wondered if that would have been possible had she been in the car during the crash. The police report stated that the front and side air bags in her car had deployed, and yet her body was far from the vehicle.

We believe that Lisa had been able to walk out of her car after the accident because the air bags protected her, and when she exited her car, she was hit by the speeding tractor trailer. It threw her body and mangled her car completely. We suspect that he struck the other two cars involved, which were near Lisa's car.

Then the tractor trailer struck the Chevy Tahoe. But something did not make sense. If the tractor trailer was going in the right direction, then why did he strike the Tahoe in the front? And why did the driver of the tractor trailer run away? Why wasn't he ever found?

We pray that one day we will know what really happened from somebody who was involved in this car accident. Maybe there is more that they can tell us.

## The Book: Boldness in Faith

The time is coming when everything will be revealed; all that is secret will be made public.

—Luke 12:2 (NLT)

While I waited for the final report, I figured out what it meant when God pushed me to "go to the public" right after my daughter's car accident.

I gradually saw the sense in it the further the case went on, but I did not want to admit it to myself. A book? Me? I thought to myself, *You are kidding me!*

English is not only my second language; it also frequently gets me into trouble, which always made my children laugh. I learned words from TV cartoons, like *Ghostbusters*, but I only used the second half of the word and had no idea that it sounded as if I were swearing. I absolutely hate swearing, and I think doing so is degrading, so this was a painful lesson for me. It was such a painful lesson that I even wrote a poem about it.

> English is my problem,
> English is this "thing"
> That makes me WOBBLE
> And breaks my ink.
> This problem is the issue
> Which I struggle to show the world
> This issue is like a tissue,
> Can be sticky to use, then fold.

Writing a book in English would be a huge and time-consuming challenge for me, but eventually, it was the only option left. It wasn't right how this case was done, so I wanted to tell this story to others. God wanted me to "go to the public," so here I am, sharing my faith, pain, struggles, and experiences. I hope it will help others who are going through tragedies like mine, who feel as if they are being deceived and taken advantage of. My message for you is that you are not alone. I hope that maybe my experience will help you by encouraging you to stay in your marriage and trust in God. Maybe you need faith because you are being confused and deceived. I didn't feel very sure of myself setting out to write this book about a mess of a car accident case and a fraudulent forensic report, but faith and trust in God guided me through this whole process. I prayed for David's boldness because I know that I am facing a giant. This giant is our "worldly system." It is the sin of human society, our greed, abusive power, and our pride, and we can choose to be "in" this worldly system or not. I believe that there are still many people who try to preserve dignity, honesty, and truth in our world. Our worldly laws are so complicated that they often look like they are at war with one another. God's laws, on the other hand, are simple and clear. Everybody can understand the Ten Commandments, which create such harmony. No one law contradicts the other. Jesus summed up the Ten Commandments in one simple law: "So now I am giving you a new commandment: Love each other. Just as I have loved you, you should love each other. Your love for one another will prove to the world that you are my disciples" (John 13:34–35, NLT).

I was thinking about how simple that is. The Bible doesn't want us Christians to be quiet. We should be God's witnesses and proclaim the good news—that God's kingdom will come soon. We should share our experiences and expose evil because if we will not do this, then who will? We should know who we are in Christ. God gave David a rock. He gave Christians a boldness in Jesus Christ to make the right choices and support each other, to speak, to share, and to write about their faith. We are equipped with what we need in order to face the giant. We have faith in Christ and this should make us strong. We have to remember that God always wins.

Jesus prayed: "I am praying not only for those disciples but also for all who will ever believe in me because of their testimony." (Jon 17:20, NLT)

Take no part in the worthless deeds of evil and
darkness; instead, rebuke and expose them.

—Ephesians 5:11 (NLT)

There is good news though. It is never too late to come
to our senses and repent to God, acknowledging that
only Jesus is our savior—not money or politics or our
possessions. It is never too late to ask him for forgiveness
for neglecting God's laws of love, "And you must love the
Lord your God with all your heart, all your soul, and all
your strength" (Deuteronomy 6:5, NLT). It's not too late to
place our hope in God.

A year after Lisa's tragic accident, on July 28, 2013, I
gathered all my notes and reports in Lisa's room and prayed.
Everything was still fresh in my memory. This is not only
about me and my family, I realized.

I believe that God sees the bigger picture that I still
am not sure I see yet. And when he is telling me to do
something, I should do it. It wasn't easy emotionally at all.
Thanks to the presence of Lisa's hand on my arm, which
was with me when I wrote this book and which is still
around, I was able to find the strength and courage to
proceed, to seek truth, to hope, to endure. In this worldly
system, when human dignity seems to be losing its value,
many families are destroyed by divorce; loyalty and love
become more seldom, and hands are hopelessly dropping.
America is always being looked to by the rest of the world.
I came to the USA for a better life like many foreigners.
Here I found a much greater treasure that I could ever
have imagined—freedom in Christ. I love America. My
daughter Lisa was born here in Boston, and we are proud
of this. No other country has such beautiful hymns like
"God bless America." I think we should sing this more
often to renew our hope in Christ and praise our God.

"Hymn of Hope"
Dana Banat

America, in hope we sing a new song,
When darkness wants to take us
And blind our eyes with wrong
We Look upon God's righteousness
We Stand strong for what is true
God blessed America abundantly
He will bless America anew

We've been through the Valley of Death
And covenants were with us
God set America Free
And those who obey Him and trust

When we are struck down and deceived
The Constitution still reminds
God set America free
And He gave sight to the blind
By His love He is healing the blind

America, in hope, we sing a new song.

The Pharisees who were standing there heard him
and asked, "Are you saying we are blind?"

"If you were blind you wouldn't be guilty," Jesus
replied. "But you remain guilty because you claim
you can see."

—John 9:40–41 (NLT)

# Memory of Wonders

And we know that God causes everything to work
together for the good of those who love God and
are called according to his purpose for them.

-Romans 8:28 (NLT)

Spring of 2012 was unusually beautiful and started early. One day that March, Lisa and I were excited to take a long walk through Borderland State Park. We usually never went there during this season, because the weather was cold and the paths in the park were muddy, but it was so nice out that we decided to go. We walked fast and laughed at how I barely kept pace with my daughter's long legs. I enjoyed listening to our laughter echo through the woods. It was beautiful and special, and we breathed in deeply the fresh, warm air, as the blue sky filtered through the still leafless branches.

Suddenly Lisa stopped.

"Did you see that?" she asked. I stopped too and looked around.

"What?" I asked. She pointed to the tree we'd just passed with the broken upper branches. On the top of the bare wood, about ten feet up, was a bird that looked like neither owl nor hawk.

"What is it?" I asked. The large bird was not afraid and didn't move, but looked at us.

I decided to investigate, and slowly, step by step, I walked toward the tree where the weird bird was sitting motionless.

"Be careful," Lisa said. I was surprised that the bird stared intensely at her, and ignored me as I approached.

"He likes you," I said to Lisa when I was six feet from him. I stopped when he shot a quick look at me. The bird was large like an owl but his appearance was more like a hawk. Before, we'd seen owls in the zoo, but they weren't like this.

"He definitely likes you," I repeated as I walked back to her. The owl remained in the same position and continued to stare at Lisa. I was amazed by this adventure and regretted leaving our cell phones in the car, which we could have snapped pictures with. We stayed looking at the bird for a while in hopes that he would move or fly away. When he did not, we eventually kept walking and left him alone. I turned back every now and then and saw that the owl was still sitting there like before.

After this experience, Lisa became subdued, and we walked quietly for a moment, enjoying each other's company. Old dry leaves rustled under our footsteps, and the sweet-smelling breeze in the forest alerted my senses that winter was over. It was calm and pleasant, and for a moment, it was as if we were a part of our wonderful surroundings.

Finally, Lisa broke the silence.

"I want to show you something," she said. "It is me and my friends' favorite place, where we always meet when we come to Borderland Park."

Lisa brought me to a stone bench on top of a small, steep hill by the lake. The bench was surrounded with trees and thick bushes, and it was private and cozy there, with a nice view of the lake. As we sat there, I noticed she was looking for something on the nearby trees.

"What are you looking for?" I asked her.

She laughed and answered, "I carved my name on one of them. In a hidden place. It was a long time ago and I forget where."

"You carved on a tree?" I asked with disbelief.

"Mom, I was younger!" she answered. For a while we both were looking, but without any luck.

After Lisa's funeral, her friends painted a big rock with their names on it. They put this rock next to this bench that Lisa had shown me. It took me a few months to go and see it, but then Ben and I started going more and more often to Borderland Park to sit on this bench and pray. It's a peaceful, relaxing place, and now it's special for us. One day when we went there, I was terrified to discover that this rock from Lisa's friends was gone.

"We have to find it!" I exclaimed to my husband.

"Dana," my husband said, trying to calm me down, "you must have known that one day this could happen." We looked on the bottom of this steep hill and on the edges of the lake but we couldn't find it. I called Lisa's friends to see if they knew anything about it. They had noticed the disappearance of the rock, and hadn't been able to find it either. They'd thought about me—that maybe I would know where it was. When Ben and I came back to this bench again, I decided to try to find it one more time. I asked God to help me and prayed that He lead me to this rock.

Ben checked the shore of the lake at the bottom of the hill again, but I went in a different direction, listening to my instinct.

"I found it!" I screamed.

"How?" Ben was amazed.

"Now we need to put this rock in a safer place so it's not so visible," I said. I chose the perfect place, close to the bench between two compact birch trees. There was a cavity between the two trees that was the perfect size for this rock. After putting it there, I stood upstraight and, at the height of my face, I noticed that between those trees, on one of them, Lisa's name was carved. For a moment, Ben and I just stared at each other in astonishment. I'd found the rock and Lisa's name.

I called Lisa's friends and we made a plan to go see this rock together. I was happy to see them for the first time since Lisa's funeral, but when we entered Borderland Park, I became suddenly overwhelmed listening to them giggle and talk excitedly; I longed to be there with Lisa, and it brought me to tears. As I started to cry, they froze with surprise. I apologized and told them that I was not ready to go there with them yet, and when I arrived back at home, I ran to Lisa's room to pray and meditate. I needed God's comfort.

A short time later, these same girls called me saying that, when I was ready, they would like to see me again. They had amazing stories about Lisa they wanted to share with me. I wanted to see them and hear about these stories, so we finally met. They told me about how much they were missing Lisa and we talked about the times we had spent with her. They wanted to tell me about the wonderful things that had happened for them, because of Lisa. They believe that she still watches over them and cares.

## Nielle

At that time, Lisa's friend Nielle was living and attending college in Boston. Her apartment was close to the place where the Boston marathon takes place every April. That past spring (2013), she and her boyfriend were standing on the street with the crowd and waiting for the marathon's runners. It was chilly and she thought of Lisa, remembering how Lisa would always nag her to take a sweater when they were going out. Lisa and Nielle are both very tall and thin, and they got cold easily.

This memory bothered her. Nielle was living so close that she could even see the marathon from her apartment window, so she decided to quickly get her sweater. Once she got into her apartment, she heard explosions and screams from the street, and knew that something bad had happened. Nielle saw from her window that smoke was rising from the place where she'd been standing with the crowd and waiting for the runners just a few minutes before. She'd been safely inside when the bombs went off. Nielle believes that the habit of always bringing a sweater, which she learned from Lisa, saved her life.

## Amanda

Lisa's close friend Amanda told me that she had a very strong longing for Lisa. She missed Lisa so much that she put her picture everywhere she could. She even had one in her car so she could talk to Lisa while she was driving. She had pictures of her and Lisa in her room, and she even had pictures of her and Lisa from when they were young on the living room coffee table next to her family pictures.

When, shortly after Lisa's accident, Amanda's house caught fire and burned down, only Amanda's room stayed safe and looked as if nothing had happened. But even more amazing was the fact that the coffee table in the living room, where the pictures of her family and of her and Lisa were, remained completely untouched by the fire. The entire living room had burned, except for the coffee table!

God did not let these pictures, which are now so precious to Amanda, perish.

Amanda told me that she wasn't home when her house burned down. At the time, she was living at college. She showed me a picture of her new friend who looks a lot like Lisa and behaves almost like her too. Amanda was surprised when she discovered that her new friend's nickname is also Lisa. It was a blessing for Amanda to meet her. I appreciated those encouraging stories that Lisa's friends shared with me. I asked them what they missed the most about Lisa, and they all agreed that she was the one who kept them together. They missed her positive, encouraging attitude and, of course, her music. We decided to keep in touch and see each other every once in a while.

> Let heaven fill your thoughts. Do not think only about things down here on earth.
>
> —Colossians 3:2

## Eric

About half a year after Lisa's funeral, I met with Eric, Lisa's boyfriend. I wanted to know if he was reading the Bible I gave him and to see how he was doing. We met in a Mexican restaurant and talked about Lisa. He told me how sorry he was and how he missed her and how he was struggling with his faith. I tried to encourage him by telling him the stories of my visions of Lisa. He also shared with me what he called a "very weird adventure." As I mentioned before, Eric was working for a landscaping company, and was assigned to cut the upper branches of a tall tree, which were too close to high-voltage power lines. These power lines had been stretched by a storm and were hanging too low above the street. While he worked trimming and cutting tree branches, he was high up on an elevated platform overlooking the road and began to think about Lisa and how she died. Suddenly, at that moment, a big tractor-trailer drove by, hitting the electrical power lines right next to him. They would have certainly killed him on the spot, but somehow, miraculously, the power lines did not reach him and he was safe. He admitted to me that he'd never been as terrified in his entire life as he was at that moment. He believes that Lisa still cares for him.

"Yes she does," I said with confidence. "Eric," I said, "we never know when the time will be that we are called to return to God. Our life is up to God, not up to us."

## Don

Don works for a stone company. I heard his tragic story before I met him at the cemetery office. He listened to my story about Lisa, but he wasn't sure about God or His love for him. The question why was always on his lips when I spoke with him. He is a very nice, gentle man and that's what everybody says about him. His marriage was very good, and he and his wife loved each other deeply. Then his wife got sick, and the illness slowly destroyed her. She was suffering for a long time before she died, and Don watched this whole process, emotionally suffering greatly. His wife had believed that God would give her back her health, but Don doubted this. Nevertheless, his wife was a faithful, good Christian to the end. Thanks to her, Don was a believer too. But he lost his faith when she passed away. Don admitted to me that he had a vision too. One night his wife appeared to him in the light, wearing a white gown, and from that moment he began his own journey to faith. He said to me, "It must be something." Hope was reawakening in Don. I was happy to be Jesus's witness for him. Ben and I pray for Don and we hope that he will again trust Jesus as his Savior; that he will understand Christ's love for him and how He suffered on the cross for our eternal life so that we will live again with Him forever; and that Don will be reunited with his wife and never suffer again.

## Peter's Full Story of Faith

Before Lisa's car accident, when Peter was still living with us, he struggled with his faith. He did go to church with us, but it was because, he said, he was obedient to us.

"After confirmation I will not go to church anymore," he announced. "How can I believe in God when there is so much evil in this world? Why would God allow evil to destroy so many innocent people, and allow those innocent people to suffer and even die?" He became angry with God more and more.

I tried to explain the story of Adam and Eve to Peter, and about how they struggled with the problem of free will. I told him how our first parents polluted our perfect human nature with sin and destroyed our relationship with the Heavenly Father, because of their disobedience. But Peter did not want to listen, and was too focused on his own theory. We were praying with Lisa for him. I would put Bible verses on the refrigerator and changed them often, and I noticed Peter would read them and become frustrated. I tried to keep reminding myself of the saying "sometimes things get worse before they get better." I had this feeling inside that something was happening.

Around this time, Peter began working with a guy named Matthew, who was quickly becoming his best friend. Mathew is a Christian and he showed Peter 1 Corinthians 13 "Love is the Greatest." Peter was amazed by how beautiful and true it is. Matthew encouraged Peter to ask me about the story of my faith and I was grateful to God for the opportunity to share the story of my vision of Jesus's face with my son.

Around this time, there was also an M. Night Shyamalan movie playing in theaters called Devil, and Peter was intrigued by it, so he went to see it. There wouldn't be any special reason for me to mention this horror movie if it hadn't changed Peter. He was surprised when a verse from the Bible appeared on the screen at the start of the movie: 1Peter 5:8,"Be careful! Watch out for attacks from the devil, your great enemy. He prowls around like a roaring lion, looking for some victim to devour." My son's name is Peter and his work number is fifty-eight, so the verse caught his attention.

He told me that he'd had a weird experience a few months before seeing this movie. He was taking a relaxing bath before work, when, for a moment, he noticed a shadow was shifting around him. It gave him a very unpleasant feeling. He suspected what it was, and because of that, he wanted to see this movie. In it, the devil was portrayed as a shadow. The moral of the movie was that wherever the devil exists, God exists also! Peter understood the message. "Mom," he said to me, "I believe in God." At this time though, he still had a problem with Jesus. He was uncertain about who Jesus really was. This was the beginning of his faith journey, two years before Lisa's car accident. It's true that's it's easier to believe in evil because we see it and are used to experiencing it often in this corrupt world. The media would rather talk about the bad things that happen than the good, and that preference is mirrored in the speech of people every day. But good exists also. We just need to see it and we can experience it in full— it is up to us. God gave us free will; we can freely choose to stay trapped in these corrupt worldly systems or rise above them, in the Kingdom of God forever.

Where do we want to be "in"?

After Lisa's car accident, we gave Peter her laptop computer. It was special to him and he did not change anything about it. He left her background picture in place— stars on a purple-and-blue sky— and he added Lisa's picture to it. After his experience with the angel, he had this need, and he searched for an image that resembled what he'd seen so he could show us what the angel had looked like. He searched mostly on the computer and in churches, but without any success. After a few months of this, he gave up. One day however, a picture of the angel suddenly appeared on his Facebook newsfeed. He told me that, when he saw it, he felt ecstatic, and the wonderful feeling he'd experienced when the angel was with him suddenly returned. "It was the right time," Peter said. "I needed this reminder." He'd been feeling depressed from missing Lisa and from other issues in his life.

It was amazing because the picture of the angel had the same background as Lisa's picture had on her laptop: stars on a purple-and-blue sky. The journey of Peter's faith is still going on and it's wonderful to see and to be part of.

## Ben

Living in the temporary work camp was a challenge. The rooms were tiny and loud, and there was not enough space in them for the winter clothes they needed. Ben had to keep his clothes packed up in suitcases under his twin bed. The real challenge was the bathroom, which Ben had to share with his coworkers. But the camp was well organized, and the rooms were warm and neatly cleaned. The service people were kind and the food was excellent. Above all, we were thankful to God for the blessing of work. I told my husband that I'd noticed all of the projects he'd been assigned to were successful and tremendously blessed. God is faithful.

When the project in Kitimat expanded and there was not enough room for new workers in the work camp, my husband's company had an extraordinary idea. They decided to transfer the camp onto a cruise ship in the Douglas Channel. Workers, including my husband, were worrying about how it would be, until Ben saw a picture that had been sent to him on the computer. The picture showed a ship under a beautiful double rainbow. Ben knew it was a sign from God that everything would be okay, and it was. On the ship, Ben was given a nice spacious room with his own bathroom. Most of all he likes the bright pink carpet on the floor. This must be Lisa, he thought. It was her favorite color. From his window, he has a beautiful view of the ocean. Lisa loved the ocean. When we'd considered moving in the past, Lisa told us, "It must be close to the ocean, because I can't live without it."

In April 2012, Lisa took me to a small beach that I'd never been to before. The weather was beautiful and warm, but it was not a time that people usually went to the beach in Massachusetts. The water was still very cold from the winter, but it was exciting to see the vast ocean and the waves rolling calmly onto the shore. The sun was bright and warm and felt pleasant on our pale skin, finally freed from heavy clothes. We enjoyed breathing in the fresh, salty ocean air. The water was clear and shone like glittering crystal in the sun. In the hot sun, I was tempted to take a dip in the ocean.

"Come in, Lisa!" I called to my daughter as I floundered on the edge of the water. When we finally did swim, we were screaming and laughing at how cold we were until finally jumping out of the freezing water like a catapult onto the beach. After that swim, the icy ocean had left our skin itchy and red, but we were proud of how brave we were for jumping in. As we ate lunch in a nearby restaurant, we laughed and both agreed that we would remember that swim.

The ocean reminds Ben of many memories of Lisa too, especially because he lives on the cruise ship now. Ben likes it there because it's more private and quieter than the work camp. After moving into the cruise ship, Ben had to go to a work seminar for a few days, which was located in a lodge deep in the woods. In the past, whenever Ben had the opportunity, he liked to show Lisa new places; so when Ben saw how beautiful the nature was at the seminar, he felt a strong longing for Lisa. He asked God for courage and to show him some sign that Lisa was still with him, like a bird or an animal ... maybe a deer. But nothing happened.

The next morning, however, when he looked out the window of his room, he saw a cat walking slowly on the porch railing. The cat wasn't afraid of him and was very cuddly, following Ben everywhere. Ben petted him and enjoyed his company for the rest of the seminar. He asked the owner of the lodge about the cat and he told Ben that no one knew where it'd come from. The owner and crew of the lodge liked this cat and decided to take care of him. Ben told me this story later when he was home. He believed that Lisa had sent him this cat, because she loved cats.

"Did this cat have a name?" I asked.

"Yes, they called him Meme," Ben answered.

"Meme!" I shouted in disbelief. "Now I definitely believe that Lisa was sending you this cat!" Meme was Lisa's first word as an infant; she called her baby quilt "Meme." She kept this quilt until she was eighteen and it had been completely and lovingly worn to tatters.

## My Not Endless Story

To find the truth is like digging the well,
In deeper it goes, more darkness is there,
But when water is found for the thirsty heart,
Then the freshness of spring gives light to the dark!

–D.B.

It's been two years now since my daughter Lisa's car accident. After my long investigation into the fraudulent medical report and talking with many lawyers and criminal investigators, it's turned out to be more like a philosophical argument than anything else. I heard from some of them that the police felt sorry for me when they first came to my house after the accident, and that is why they were telling me that Lisa was innocent. I don't believe this is true, and it would also be against the law. Everything that the state police officer told me he repeated to my thirty-two year old son, my sister, and her brother-in-law. It seemed to me that the attorneys I met with couldn't help me to find the evidence I was interested in. A few of them admitted to me that they were Christians too, but they had their families to feed and my case was not right for them. Some suggested asking for another medical report, but how could another medical report have possibly been produced when no autopsy was done? I didn't want them to send me another fraud.

Lisa's case opened my eyes to the kind of world we live in. We've heard a lot of bad stories, but we've been used to hearing them from childhood; without experiencing these tragedies ourselves, we never really understood or felt them. It's just like how somebody who is full would not understand the experience of somebody who is dying of hunger, because he hasn't gone through the same pain. That is why we should do what is right and not just what we feel like doing. I was glad to be a Christian witness in every lawyer's office I visited. On November 15, 2013, I wrote and sent a report about the fraudulent forensic toxicology report to the following authorities: Office of the Attorney General in Massachusetts, the Boston division of the FBI and the FBI Headquarters in Washington, DC, the United States Department of Justice (fraud - Crime) in Washington, DC, the National Center for Disaster Fraud (NCDF), and more. On April 3, 2014, I also sent this report to the Governor of Massachusetts. I asked him to take the fraudulent medical report out of my daughter Lisa's accident file. I did not ask for anything else; I only wanted to clear her name. Unfortunately, I got one letter from the FBI stating that they could not help me, and I received a few phone calls from other offices telling me to wait and they would soon be in touch with me.

For me, it would be a miracle if something finally happen. The sudden silence in this matter makes me think that I will not go any further with this, and God knows it. This is why I received a message from Him at the beginning of this case to "go to the public."

I remember hearing a message from a respected preacher on TBN that fifty percent of the taxpayers in the US are Christians! If this is the truth, then there must be among them some leaders, lawyers, doctors, policemen, politicians, and journalists.

Although I tried to contact some of them, I struggled to find any help. Some of them said religion had nothing to do with it. I am so glad that our Heavenly Father has a different opinion about our troubles and is leading me through all of my human issues, and before I became a Christian, He died for my sins, which weren't religion issues at all.

> And so, since God in His mercy has given us this
> wonderful ministry, we never give up. We reject all
> shameful and underhanded methods. We do not
> try to trick anyone, and we do not distort the word
> of God. We tell the truth before God, and all who
> are honest know that.
>
> −2 Corinthians 4:1–2 (NLT)

We are all afraid to be hurt, myself included. But God is testing us on how strong we can stand for Him, how obedient we are, how well we care for each other. It is not about feeling but about doing right and trusting Him. I think we should act like Jesus's followers, always and everywhere.

My last wonderful story is simple and can be anyone's too. Earlier I wrote about Ben's aunt who lives in Germany and lost her daughter Lola. When Lola died, she left her three children, three girls for her husband Martin to raise. After our tragedy, we spoke with the aunt who'd gotten sick in order to encourage her; she was very angry with God and blamed him for what happened. After that, I did not talk with her for quite some time. A year passed by and my husband received bad news from his cousin who lives in Germany. Lola's husband Martin died suddenly at age forty-nine, and Lola's three girls are now orphans, living with Ben's uncle and aunt, their grandparents. I felt really sorry for them. It had to have been shocking for Jasmine, the youngest daughter, who was only eighteen at the time, when in the morning after preparing breakfast she went to her father's room and found him dead. I was afraid to call Ben's aunt, thinking that she would probably be even angrier than before, but I also knew that it was the right thing to do. I had to call or my conscience would not have been at peace. To my surprise, Ben's aunt was very glad that I called her and she did not understand why the rest of her family had not contacted her yet.

"Aunt, you scared them when you were grieving after your daughter Lola died," I said. "I understand. You know I do." We talked about God and prayed, and she seemed to be at peace. She told me that she envied my faith.

"You don't have to envy me," I said. "You have the same faith; I can see that. You pray, you believe in Jesus, you have peace. One thing you have to do is share it with your family, your friends, neighbors, anybody. You see, God gave me a wonderful gift when I called you. He let me see that my seeds are growing." I told my aunt that Jasmine could come visit us and stay however long she needs.

My story of faith will not end until my Lord calls me home, but for now I will share my faith with anybody and I will not be discouraged or ashamed of it. I will not confine my faith within the walls of my church; this is who I am now.

I cried so hard and for so long after Lisa passed away that I developed a hernia, and the pain was awful. I met four doctors who all gave me the same options: I could live with this, or I could have surgery to repair it, which would be best. They all agreed that it was just at the beginning stages. I was scheduled for surgery, but I still had no peace with that. Something was wrong. My surgeon was encouraging me, saying that the procedure was a "piece of cake," but I commented in frustration, "Maybe for you yes, but not for me."

I was praying and asking Jesus to heal me and I didn't understand why He wasn't doing it. On the computer I found some information and I spent a lot of time learning about my problem. At this time, my sister-in-law, Silvia, called to tell me about a health issue she was experiencing, and she told me about a Christian natural healer named Anna. I called her and she said she couldn't help me, but she promised that she would talk with somebody she trusted who knew more about this kind of problem.

"You should pray for answers and I will pray for you too!" she said to me. After a week I got an email from her. "You should exercise," she wrote. I canceled the surgery and trusted God. I learned about healthy eating and proper exercises recommended for this problem. I lost another few pounds. Though I was excited by this, it was really a sacrifice and required discipline every single day. Obstinacy and the belief that I would be healthy again helped me to persevere with being disciplined. After a few months, I saw results. The problem has almost disappeared at this point and I don't feel it anymore, but I still continue with this recovery program.

I don't have to ask God why He did not magically heal me on the spot; I know the answer. I would not have learned anything, and would not have become disciplined. By being forced to focus on recovering, it was much easier for me to start changing. I realized that if I had not changed my attitude towards my mourning, my health would have fallen apart, because I observed some more strange symptoms in different areas of my body. Every time I am missing Lisa, I repeat to myself, "Accept and be happy that she is in Heaven!"

Discipline is not only helping me physically but it is strengthening me emotionally too. I focus on Jesus and say, "I can do it, Jesus. Yes, I can." One Sunday morning in July 2014, before I went to church, I was sitting on our back porch drinking my favorite tea and reading about heaven in the Bible (John 14:2-3). It was beautiful and refreshing. The sun had just come out and a new day had begun. The brilliant pink flowers on my porch were especially conspicuous, and, for a while, I enjoyed just looking at them. I thought to myself that if I kept looking at them for a long enough time, they would become ordinary and boring. So, even when we're in heaven surrounded by the most beautiful things, it can become boring once we're accustomed to it?

And then suddenly, for a moment, I saw how this flower seemed to be changing colors and shape, and I heard this delicate sound. The grass below was waving under the gentle touch of wind and as the waving movement rippled through the green grass, it was changing its tint. I heard in my head, "Heaven never will be boring." Indeed, I beheld this vision and was hypnotized. It was wonderful! Heaven never will be boring, for sure.

A fellow church member told me, "You need these visions so much!"

"Yes, I do," I answered. "God knows what we all need and has a reason for everything." I believe there's a reason for this book, and though I would rather have my daughter alive with me more than anything else in the world, it is God who rules and I am thankful for everlasting life in heaven. This short life passes quickly and nobody knows when it is their time. I am learning to look at my daughter's passing from a heavenly perspective: now she is alive, and I am the one who is dying in this dying world, closer every day. She is more alive than I am here. I will go to her when I am finally called home to God in heaven.

God has a reason that He still is keeping me here in this world, and I submit to His will. He saved me many times when I was a kid and clearly reminded me of this later when I became a Christian. He saved me in the most vulnerable time of my life.

This story happened early in my childhood and was also a favorite story of my daughter's. My mom had a young boyfriend named Bob from an intelligent and prestigious family. Bob was an only son and his parents were not happy that he was dating my mom. I understood and heard that it was because of the many children she had, and also because she wasn't a good influence for him. For this reason, my mother and Bob planned to eliminate some of us kids, and I was one of the unlucky ones. I was quiet and very shy, and my younger sister was more like my mom was, so they wanted to keep her. While I pretended to be busy playing on the floor near them, I overheard them planning.

They planned that Bob would take me and my siblings to the meadow where the deep brook was. I should mention that this brook had a very bad reputation. It divided our village from the train station, where the village bar was located. Often people went to the bar after work and stayed there for a very long time past dark. When completely drunk and sometimes singing loudly, they liked to take the shortcut home, and instead of going over the only bridge in the village, they often crossed the brook via a wooden beam thrown across it. Some of them were not lucky and drowned. Sometimes, when we were playing near that brook, people came and drowned their kittens there. It was very brutal for us to see that as children.

Their plan was to send me over the brook on the wooden beam, to the other side where the meadow was. I had never done that before because it was forbidden to us kids; it was the village's rule. When I heard them talking, I was terrified, and I decided not to go on that beam no matter what. The next day, in the morning when most people went to work, Bob took us to the meadow and told me to go over the beam first. I didn't want to go, so he showed me how easy it was. He walked back and forth on the round wood, encouraging me to do the same, first nicely, then demandingly. When I stubbornly refused to go, he angrily put me on it himself. I slid along it carefully, ready to grab the wood if I felt my feet slipping. When I was in the middle, Bob shook the beam. I was able to remain standing, but I crouched and got ready to hang on. He shook it again and I held on for dear life, hanging above the dark deep water. I felt how fast my strength was escaping me, and I was afraid that I would soon drown like those kittens.

At that moment, I realized that it was a beautiful summer day, and that the sun was bright and the sky was very blue. I was conscious of Bob still shaking the beam, but I prayed to God to rescue me, and in my panic, I began searching the vivid, sunny meadow for anybody who might help me. In the distance I saw a small, dark dot growing rapidly, and I yelled, "Somebody is coming! Somebody is coming!"

Bob stopped shaking the beam and tried to see in the same direction I was looking. A man was coming toward us. Bob tried to help me, but I did not trust him, and with all my power, I did not let go of the beam. The man came straight over to us.

"Can I help you?" he asked politely, looking directly at me.

"No, thank you," Bob said, pulling me safely from the wood and putting me on the ground.

"Are you sure?" he asked again, still looking at me.

I felt embarrassed. He was a handsome young man and he was wearing a black suit with a white shirt. Nobody wears such elegant black suits in the morning while walking through the meadow during a normal work day. My mom and Bob were puzzled by this. They checked in church to see if there was a funeral or wedding or anything else, but nothing was happening in the village at this time. They talked about this man for a long time, trying to understand why, after our meeting, he hadn't continued his walk but had instead turned back in the direction he'd come from. Whatever the reason for it, Mom and Bob didn't plan anything like that anymore. I was safe.

This story reminds me that everybody has their time on this Earth, and God is in control. Jesus did not die and suffer to save our mortal, sinful body, but to save our eternal soul. Now I feel and understand that we are all spiritual beings in temporary, human bodies.

Jesus is the one who can save the soul for eternity. When trusting and believing in Him, we can chose to overcome any temptations. What kind of a task do our souls have in our mortal body? The task is love your Creator, your God, first, and your neighbors as yourself (Mark 12:29–30 NLT). Only the Bible, especially the New Testament, has all of the instructions, stories, and the wisdom about how to do it. This life is short, and the older we get, the more we feel how quickly time passes by. Once while reading Our Daily Bread, a nice statement under the title "Do No Harm" stuck out to me. I learned from it that the ancient Greek physician Hippocrates is credited with writing the moral oath for medical doctors to "do no harm." From the Bible's principles, Jesus is teaching us more than "do no harm." He is teaching us to love each other. It is important to remember that Jesus conquered evil and gave us the choice to be free from any of evil's traps. We are free in Christ.

It is important to keep our eyes on Jesus always so that we will not be deceived. It is important to not give up on ourselves so that we will be able to help others. It is important to easily forgive, to know that the burden of this life will be lightened by Christ. It is important to remember Jesus's message that the kingdom of heaven is near.

It is important to remember that this life is temporary, and that we'll all die one day. Are you afraid? You will live if you believe in Jesus Christ, our Rock and Redeemer! He is resurrected, and so you will be too.

I love you, my beloved daughter, Lisa. Soon we will be reunited, forever.

# Amen

It's enough to know Jesus—to know you, God,
Thank you for your life you gave on Golgotha,
for me and for others, My Lord
Thank you for never ever giving up on me,
Thank you for your love in Jesus to see.

—D. B.

## Conclusion: Delivery from Heaven

### Peter's Vision: August 4, 2014 (Monday)

Ben came home from his work rotation on Saturday, August 2, 2014. When Peter picked him up from the airport and drove him home, they had almost an hour to talk while en route, and they enjoyed chatting together. After not seeing each other for a long time, there is always a lot of catching up and discussing to do. When Ben arrived home, he spoke to me with admiration about how our son's relationship with God was growing, and how quickly he was learning discipline and self-control. Peter shared some ideas with us that God had given to him through other people, and told us about how he was praying for strength for any future trials he might face. He told me that the number 58 still had a different kind of significance for him now. It is like a warning of when temptation is coming.

The following Sunday after Ben arrived, we all were longing for Lisa, and we were sharing our thoughts and struggles concerning her. Peter is missing her a lot and thinking about her all the time. He misses the special inside jokes that only brother and sister can have that make them laugh together. Ben admits that he is still struggling to "let her go" and he hopes in vain that God will give her back to him.

I was the worst. After so many visions and signs, my longing for Lisa was still very painful and strong. I was struggling to accept her absence, and despite logic, I would have liked to believe in lies that she was alive. It's faith that always keeps me strong and grounded.

On Monday, our whole family met for breakfast: Peter, me, Ben, and Lisa's hand on my arm.

"She is with us," I said. Peter's face lit up.

"I got a delivery from heaven! From Lisa!" he said.

"What do you mean?" I asked.

"Tonight I got a delivery from heaven, and it was kind of funny and happy." Ben and I both stopped breathing for a moment, and our eyes lit up with hope. Peter said that he was in some vast, desert-like place with a being that looked like a clear, transparent mound, approximately the size of a big door, but with the same size length and width. This being was so transparent that it was hard to distinguish its form and Peter could see through him. He was iridescent inside, as if full of rainbow color: yellow, orange, greenish-blue and white. He talked to Peter with a style much like Lisa's when she used to joke with him.

The being said to Peter, "You will have a delivery from heaven, from Lisa! It will be a package, or may be there will be nothing there." Peter knew that there would be something there, and that he was just joking like Lisa would. The being said, "Don't be afraid."

At that moment, Peter saw another being fly like a rocket at full speed down from heaven toward him, and he was carrying a package. Because he'd been warned to not be afraid, Peter calmly watched as his delivery shot like an arrow and ripped through the air, which began to look like foaming water. The package landed on the ground at Peter's feet, and the courier immediately returned to heaven, with the same cosmic speed.

The package looked like an ordinary brown box. Peter felt that, as he was slowly and carefully opening the box, the heavenly being who'd spoken with him was watching with joyful excitement, like a kid opening Christmas presents. This excitement was contagious, and Peter soon felt the same way. Inside of the box, a pail of bright yellow sand hung in the air, and on top of it was Lisa's perfect footprint. When Peter woke up, he felt as if he hadn't been sleeping, and he knew it was real.

We were very surprised to hear about this delivery, but it soon made sense to us too. We began talking about what it meant to us.

"I think it means that Lisa is in heaven and she is having a good time! It makes me feel better," Peter said.

"And she lives by the ocean! And she has a body, because ghosts can't make footprints on sand," I added.

"I have to let her go," Ben said. "She will not come back. She is walking on heavenly ground now."

After this delivery from Lisa, my intense longing for her began to change. I still miss her, and I will for the rest of my life, but with a different attitude. I have to remember that this separation is temporary, and I am learning to accept that she is in heaven and she is happy. We all have to accept that.

I planned to finish this book with chapter 7, and on Sunday evening, the day after Ben came home, I just finished the last page of this chapter. On Monday, our son, Peter, brought us this news about his dream vision, his "delivery from heaven, from Lisa." For me, it was like a stamp or a seal sent to us for this book, a sign that it is finished, "amen" (it means approval).

I think that God wants me to add this event to my book, so we can clearly understand His message, so I started writing this concluding chapter 8 (number 8 is my husband's favorite number and became our family's too). The day after Ben came home, we wrote a list with a plan for what we would do for the next two weeks he was home. The first thing we'd planned, before Ben had even come home yet, was that we would go to our family's favorite beach: Horse Neck. We wanted to go there for a long walk if the weather was right for us— mostly cloudy and not too hot— and that weather happened the day after Peter's vision, on Tuesday. As we walked on the beach, Ben and I talked about Peter's news. Ben said with wonderment that he never would have guessed what was inside that package. I believe that Lisa knew how difficult it would be for us to go to this beach because of the memory of her. I think one of the many reasons that she sent this footprint to us was to encourage us to go to this beach, because as we go ahead with our lives here on Earth, we should enjoy it. We had a very pleasant, long walk.

For the rest of this week, we talked about and contemplated this wonderful delivery from Lisa. We wondered if the heavenly being was like the arc of a rainbow, and we also wondered if it was Lisa who'd welcomed Ben home with a rainbow. It was special to us that this vision was given to us through our son, Peter.

That next Saturday, Peter and his fiancée, Nicole, went to a restaurant for dinner, and he told her about his vision that he'd had that Monday. After dinner, they came home and went on the computer to check their emails. Nicole saw a picture posted on her Facebook newsfeed of a footprint in the sand with the following caption: "Accept what is, let go of what was, and have faith in what will be."

"Peter!" she yelled with excitement. "Look!" She was witnessing Peter's vision. The being from heaven had told Peter sarcastically, "Maybe there will be nothing there." Nicole and Peter were very surprised to see it online. The message that had been invisible in the box was now clearly written on the photo of the footprint in the sand.

When I was thinking about Peter's vision and how it all happened, I realized that a footprint in the sand was the perfect sign for this season in August, the best time to go to the beach, and Lisa's favorite time of the year. The vision happened on a Sunday night, just at the beginning of Ben's two week rotation home from work in Canada. It also happened that Canada was celebrating Family Day the next day, when our family was meeting for breakfast. All of these events were not a coincidence. The message first appeared in Peter's dream; then it was clarified a week later when it showed up again on Facebook. God still rules and is in control. He still has a plan for us. Hope and trust in Jesus will live in us for as long as we shall live. Keeping our eyes always on Jesus helps us to focus on a Godly perspective for our future. This can strengthen our faith, which needs to be exercised practically in our everyday choices (WWJD?). Philippians 2:5 (NLT) says, "Your attitude should be the same that Christ Jesus had." And we should practice spiritually, through our prayers. Thessalonians 5:17 (NLT) says, "Pray without ceasing." And we should read the Bible daily; it will help us to understand God's will for us. It will help our faith grow and strengthen our relationship with God. Be ready: always be content and faithful while waiting, because we never know when our Lord Jesus will come.

> If we love our Christian brothers and sisters, it
> proves that we have passed from death
> to eternal life.
>
> —1 John 3:14 (NLT)

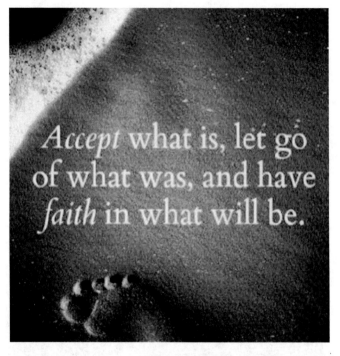

# NOTE FROM THE AUTHOR

I was like everybody else. I didn't think that this kind of tragedy would ever happen to me. I believed that my family and I were true Christians and that after my vision of Jesus's face I had a special relationship with our Heavenly Father. When others experienced awful tragedies, I hurt for them, but I thanked God for His love and for His protection of my family.

But I was wrong.

I am not better than others. The closer our relationship with the Heavenly Father, the more responsibility we have to follow Jesus Christ, our wonderful savior. When we don't want to take the next step, God will move us. Not because He wants to hurt us, but because He is saving us. When we believe that everything has a purpose, and we understand that this life is temporary and our home is in Heaven, we don't have to be afraid of anything and this news is a great joy. We will respect God and His will for us. We should live in the truth so that we may glorify our God, and we should follow Jesus Christ everywhere and anywhere—in our homes and our workplaces where we spend so much of our lives.

After I finished this book, I still struggled to see the big picture of it clearly. I was not looking to blame anybody for what happened. I understand now that it was God's will through this book to show me and others in a practical way, through my daughter's case, what it means to live with faith and practice it boldly in our everyday lives.

Jesus affirmed to Pilate that He is a king. He said, "I was born for that purpose. And I came to bring truth to the world.

All who love the truth recognize that what I say is true."

"What is truth?" Pilate asked. He did not recognize the truth. If he had, he would have done his job and would not have let Jesus be crucified, because he knew that Jesus was innocent. To be Christian means to follow Christ and always stand up for the truth. It is important to do our jobs like Christians, and be a Christian in every aspect of our lives, not just while we are at church. The charity we give and good deeds we do in church will not save us; it is good to give, but if we do not live for God in our everyday lives, we are not truly following Christ.

I understand now that God's love is better than anything else and can overcame any evil, especially fear. If God made sure that innocent baby Jesus fulfilled his purpose in his life for us, why should we be afraid that God wouldn't do it for his children in Christ.

Our only thanks is to trust God—our Heavenly Father, when living in harmony and peace for His glory. Through Christ we all should love one another, and can show this by standing boldly for the truth and boldly supporting each other while waiting for our Lord to come again. He will come!

# LOVE IS THE GREATEST

1 Corinthians 13: 1-8,13 (NLT)
IF I could speak in any language in heaven or on earth
but didn't love others, I would only be making meaning-
less noise like a loud gong or a clinging cymbal.

If I had the gift of prophecy, and if I knew all the
mysteries of the future and knew everything about
everything, but didn't love others, what good would I be?

And if I had the gift of faith so that I could
speak to a mountain and make it move, without
love  I would be no good to anybody.

If I gave everything I have to the poor and even
sacrificed my body, I could boast about it; but if I
didn't love others, I would be of no value whatsoever.

*Love is patient and kind.*
*Love is not jealous or boastful or proud or rude.*
*Love does not demand its own way.*
*Love is not irritable, and it keeps no record*
*of when it has been wronged.*
*It is never glad about injustice but rejoices*
*whenever the truth wins out.*
*Love never gives up, never loses faith,*
*is always hopeful, and endures through every circumstance.*
*Love will last forever,[...]*

There are three things that will endure - faith, hope,
- and the greatest of those is Love.


- GOD  IS  LOVE -

# SHARING JESUS'S LOVE

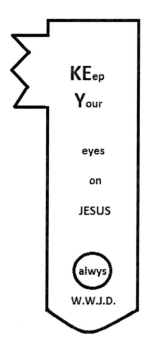

A portion from the sale of this book will be given to non-profit organizations dedicated to helping orphans.

For more information about the organizations these donations will benefit, please visit:

www.Lbanat-truthbetoldusa.com

The rest of the proceeds from this book will go to the ministry of "Sharing Jesus's Love"